Salvo

Pick a few + on
birthday we'll go and

i love you ♡

Ale xxx

07·10·2017

Whisky

obsessions

John Lamond

John Lamond is a Master of Malt and author of several books including *The Malt Whisky File*. He contributes to international consumer magazines and industry journals, has conducted whisky tastings worldwide and lectured for Wine & Spirit Education Trust for over twenty years. He also created the Scotch Whisky Trail Certificate Course, the world's first Scotch whisky evening class.

Whisky

obsessions

John Lamond

hardie grant books

Contents

Why be obsessed with whisky?

Whisky is the greatest drink in the world; the stuff of legend, of healing, of friendship and companionship. In Gaelic it was literally 'the water of life'. No other spirit offers such elegance, such complexity or such value. And with all the excellent choices available, no one should have to settle for a whisky they don't enjoy. It just starts with knowing what is out there.

Scotch whisky is spelt 'whisky' (plural 'whiskies'), the primary spelling we will use in this book, and must be from Scotland to be called scotch. The Irish spirit – which has an even longer history – is spelt 'whiskey' (plural 'whiskeys'). This spelling is also used in the USA, with its ryes and bourbons first brewed by pioneering settlers from Scotland and Ireland.

There is an enthusiasm about whisky today that did not exist 30 years ago, and that has enabled a great deal of research into what goes on inside the cask. As a result, the quality of spirit now being bottled has never been higher. The boutique distilleries, in particular, are benefiting from this new research and knowledge, as they are able to experiment with small amounts of spirit and unusual casks, and so they in turn impart new information to the large distilleries. Thus within an already wide range of whisky, there are different ages, finishes and experimental bottlings for you to sample and enjoy.

▲ A good whisky is a snapshot of the seasons from the year it was distilled; the range of flavours on offer is vast and tantalizing.

Generally, but not necessarily, the younger a whisky, the coarser, more cerealy flavoured it is going to be, as it has not yet had time to lose its hard and youthful rough edges nor had time to assimilate softer, mature, oak characters. Some whiskies, such as Glen Grant or Glenfiddich, only start to come into their own after 18 years, while bourbons, Canadian or American ryes, Indian or Australian whiskies, because of their warmer maturation conditions, mature relatively quickly. In fact, it is very unusual for these to survive in the cask much longer than 15 years simply because of the heat. If one of these hot-country whiskies has been bottled in excess of 15 years of age, you can be sure that particular care has been taken over these casks while they aged, as the company's reputation hangs on your appreciation of their whiskies.

Aged whisky is valuable. Glenfiddich 50 Years Old, for example, is only the second vatting (the term for the blending process) ever made. The first was produced from nine casks laid down between 1937 and 1939 by Glenfiddich founder David Grant – one for each of his grandchildren as a thank you for helping him build the distillery. The usual retail price for a bottle today is about £22,850. Another very valuable whisky is the Dalmore 62 Years Old, a bottle of which sold for a mere £125,000 in 2011. Only 12 bottles were produced and one of these was bought – and drunk – during one evening in a hotel bar in London in 2005. Should you acquire one, please give me a shout when you open the bottle if you feel in need of some good company.

These are unique and special products often made by craftsmen decades ago. An old vintage cannot be repeated and will be a biography of the seasons of that year. Therefore the range of flavours available in whisky is tantalizing. At one end of the spectrum there is the delicate, unpeated Glengoyne where the barley is air dried. The flavour is of green apples and sweet liquorice turning to linseed and almonds; at the other there is the huge smoky, seaweed pungency of Laphroaig. In between we have a whole rainbow of styles from shortbread to syrup to Asian spices to smoked trout. In this book I have picked out some of the great whiskies of today, my personal favourites from all over the world, for you to savour and enjoy.

1

Fundamentals

Whisky ingredients

Whisky is made from three basic ingredients –
grain, yeast and water – and the process of making
it is relatively straightforward. Each distillery
combines the raw materials using tried and tested
production techniques.

Grain

Whisky is made from the cereal grains barley, corn,
rye and wheat, and the grain used defines the
characteristics of the whisky. Most barley grown
today is used in the production of whisky and
beer. Single malt whisky is made from 100 per cent
fully malted grains of barley. All other whiskies are
produced from a mix of different proportions of these
four grains.

Yeast

During production, yeast is added to the porridge-
like mash and feeds on its sugars, transforming them
into alcohol and carbon dioxide. There are many
kinds of distillers' and brewers' yeasts and each will
have a different effect on a whisky's character.

Water

Every distillery needs a plentiful local source of water
because it is added and removed at different stages
throughout a whisky's production. In Kentucky, most
water is hard, having been filtered through limestone,
which adds minerals to the water, making enzyme

action during the mashing process more efficient as well as influencing the flavour formation. Water in the Scottish Highlands is mostly soft, flowing through granite as well as over peat and heather. Soft water has a low calcium content that enables the yeast added during fermentation to make a strong start.

Wood

Not strictly an ingredient, but the wood used to make the casks in which whisky matures influences the spirit's complexity. Many experts argue that during maturation the cask contributes up to 70 per cent of the flavour and character of a whisky. The wood used for casks today is mainly American white oak. For a whiskey to be deemed bourbon it has to be matured in new casks of white oak, from which the spirit extracts vanillin from the wood, giving a sweet vanilla note. Bourbon casks are also charred to different levels enabling the spirit to access fully the flavours in the semi-porous wood. Scottish, Irish and Japanese distilleries reuse bourbon and sherry casks during maturation.

Peat

Peat is partially carbonized plant material that is usually found in waterlogged areas. Water that flows over peat absorbs some of its characteristics but not as much as a whisky made from barley that has been malted over burning peat, which brings distinctive earthy and smoky aromas and flavours. In Scotland some peats include seaweed that gives a salty, iodine characteristic to a spirit.

Making whisky

The main stages of making whisky – malting, mashing, fermentation, distillation and maturation – have remained unchanged for generations.

Malting

The first step in whisky production is to soak barley in water for several days and then spread it out on the malting floor. When the grains start to germinate, known as the 'green malt', they are transferred to the kiln, at exactly the appropriate time, where a higher temperature prevents further germination. This step retains the grains' starch content, which will be turned into sugars at the next stage of production. Some distilleries in Scotland, Ireland and Japan dry the barley over burning peat that adds to the aromas and flavours of the finished whisky. The malted barley is then milled to coarse flour known as 'grist'.

Malt whisky is made from 100 per cent malted barley while grain whisky may contain a percentage of malted barley. Today, commercial malting companies usually undertake the malting process, often producing malted barley to a distillery's exact specification. A few distilleries in Scotland still malt their own barley (such as Bowmore, see page 52, 54–55).

Mashing

The grist is mixed with hot water to form a mash that is then stirred at high temperatures releasing

▲ Whisky barrels stacked at Aberlour Glenlivet distillery, Strathspey, Scotland.

enzymes that convert the grains' starch to sugars, which dissolve into the hot water. The remaining liquid (now called the 'wort') cools and is drained into large wooden or steel vessels.

Fermentation

As the wort enters the fermenting vessel, yeast is added. Fermentation begins, rapidly converting the sugars in the wort into alcohol. The wort, now known as the 'wash', contains around 7 to 10 per cent alcohol and is ready for distillation.

Distillation

The process of distillation can take place in either a pot still or a column still. Because alcohol boils at a lower temperature than water, the wash is heated and the spirit is drawn off as a vapour that rises into a condenser. The alcohol is then condensed back into a liquid that is collected.

Pot still distillation

Malt whisky is distilled in a pot still. It is twice – sometimes three times – distilled in stills that look like big copper onions. The copper helps the separation of the spirit from the water. In the first distillation, the heating cooks out the crude alcohols and other elements. The results, known as 'low wines', are passed into the spirit still, similar in shape but smaller than the pot still because it does not need to deal with the same quantities. Low wines contain 21 per cent alcohol. The second distillation produces three distinct condensates: the first of these is called 'foreshots' or 'heads', the second is the 'heart' and the last is called 'feints' or 'tails'. Foreshots are very high in strength (75 to 80 per cent alcohol) and mildly toxic containing some methanol, while the feints are low in alcohol. Foreshots and feints go back into the pot still to lend character to the next batch of distillation. The heart (containing between 63 and 72 per cent alcohol) goes into casks for maturation.

Column still distillation

Grain whisky is produced in a column still (often known as a continuous or patent still). The continuous still was patented in 1830 by Aeneas Coffey, a former Inspector-General of Excise in Ireland. Grain whisky distillation is much more efficient: it produces far greater volumes than pot still distillation but produces a more refined, less characterful spirit and so tends to be used for blends mixed with small amounts of malt whisky. Grain whisky will often use a mix of malted and unmalted barley and other grains such as maize, rye or wheat.

▶ Copper whisky stills at the Glenkinchie distillery, located in the Lowlands of Scotland, near Edinburgh.

Bourbon, rye, Tennessee and Canadian whiskey, and the grain spirit for blending Scotch whiskies are distilled in column stills.

Maturation

At this stage the spirit, called the 'new make', must mature in an oak cask for a minimum of three years before it can be called Scotch whisky.

Scotch whisky is matured in oak casks that have previously contained bourbon or sherry and the residues within these casks affect the flavour and colour of the maturing spirit. Sometimes port, Madeira or rum casks have been used for maturation and some distillers have even experimented with Sauternes and claret casks. The expansion and contraction of the cask due to seasonal changes in temperature affects the spirit's maturation. Some harsh spirit flavours may be exhaled through the semi-porous oak cask while the natural aromas of the local environment, such as seaweed or salty sea air, can be absorbed into the cask.

As a whisky matures, evaporation also causes the cask to lose alcoholic strength and volume, and to absorb oxygen through the cask. The amount of whisky lost during maturation depends on the temperature and humidity, and the microclimate within the warehouse where maturation takes place. In high temperatures, the whisky absorbs the flavours from the cask more rapidly.

Casks are often left considerably longer than three years before the bottler decides that it is ready to be blended and bottled. Most single malts, for example, mature for at least 8 to 15 years before bottling. Bourbons and ryes, however, are ready after two years.

How strong is whisky?

Alcohol by volume (ABV) is the standard used worldwide to measure the amount of alcohol (as a percentage) in an alcoholic beverage. During distillation the alcohol level varies enormously. The foreshots, for example, are high in strength, about 75–80 per cent ABV, and are set aside to be used in the next distillation. After distillation the new make is about 70 per cent ABV. In Scotland, the spirit is diluted with water to 63 per cent ABV before being put in casks for maturation. American whiskey is barrelled at 53–55 per cent ABV while in Ireland it is 62–75 per cent ABV. As the whisky matures, alcohol and water evaporate which is called the 'angels' share' in Scotland. After emptying a cask, the dregs are called the 'devil's cut'. After maturation a cask's strength may vary from 57–65 per cent ABV. Some powerful cask strength whiskies are available. Most whisky is diluted to 40 per cent ABV before bottling.

Types of whisky

SINGLE MALT
Distilled from 100 per cent malted barley, a single malt is always the product of one distillery.

BLENDED MALT WHISKY
A blend of two or more single malt whiskies.

GRAIN WHISKY
Contains unmalted barley or other malted and unmalted grains. It has a smoother and lighter flavour. Used mainly for blending.

BLENDED SCOTCH WHISKY
A blend of a single malt and grain whiskies from different distilleries.

IRISH WHISKEY

Column stills and pot stills are both used in distillation. The pot still mash has 40 to 45 per cent malted barley. Irish whiskey is triple distilled and matured for three years.

BOURBON WHISKEY

The mash is legally required to have at least 51 per cent corn grain. Bourbon must be matured in new, charred white oak barrels for two years.

TENNESSEE WHISKEY

A bourbon-style spirit that undergoes filtration through sugar maple charcoal.

RYE WHISKEY

Made from a mash of not less than 51 per cent rye. Matured in charred oak barrels.

CANADIAN WHISKEY

Mostly rye blended with a neutral base spirit. Bourbon or corn whiskey may be blended. Matured for a minimum of three years in pre-used casks.

Appreciating whisky

The more whisky you taste the better you will be able to appreciate its aromas and flavours. With practice, you will also be able to identify the country of the oak barrel, associate certain fruity notes with a particular distillery or even detect a change of distiller.

Consider the colour

▼ An elegantly pale Caol Ila 12 Year Old single malt whisky.

Hold up the glass and look at the colour. Colour gives a clue to the type of cask used; a pale gold suggests the whisky was matured in bourbon casks while darker colours indicate sherry casks. Swirl the whisky around the glass so it coats the sides, watch how the liquid runs down the side of the glass (known as the 'legs'). This give a clue to its age and style. An aged and full-bodied whisky will have longer legs than a younger, lighter-bodied style.

Use your nose

Your nose is a far more sensitive organ than your palate. Distillers sometimes work only with their nose rather than taste. Smell or 'nose' the whisky and note what you experience: has the aroma the sweetness of malt, is it smoky and fragrant, or is it salty and seaweedy?

Training your palate

The taste of a whisky should confirm everything your nose has already told you. Take a sip of the whisky neat and let your mouth feel the whisky's body: is it big, rich, creamy, smooth, soft or gentle? There are no right or wrong tastes. We each have a unique palate and we all taste things differently.

Although each cask imposes a slightly different fingerprint on its contents, the core characteristics of a distillery are there in every bottle. Highland Park, for example, always smells distinctly of honey, heather and vanilla; Glenrothes has notes of orange, honey and butterscotch; while Caol Ila has embers of burnt heather roots on the shoreline. Each of these flavours should be identifiable with a little practice. Experiment to identify and enjoy them yourself.

Savouring the finish

The lingering flavour of a whisky in the mouth after it has been swallowed is called the 'finish'. Think about a whisky's aftertaste. Does the maltiness and smokiness linger? Is there a long lingering finish? Is the finish short and crisp? You are left with a moment to think before writing a tasting note, the only way to remember your response to a whisky.

Serving whisky

Whisky deserves care, attention and delicacy in its serving. Even a blend often contains whiskies created decades ago by artisans who are now no longer with us. A single malt is the epitome of that distillery's production, and so deserves respect and reverence. While a good-sized tumbler may suffice for every day, the best whisky deserves the best glassware.

The right glass

The glass should be large enough to take a good measure so that the aromas gather above the liquid in the bowl. The spirit should breathe. You should be

▶ The right glass can make all the difference. From left to right: the humble tumbler, the Glencairn whisky glass and the Vinum single malt glass by Riedel.

able to smell all the subtleties released in the pouring. Glass is the first choice for the obvious reason that it allows you to appreciate the mellow depths of colour in what you are drinking. Recently fashions have moved away from traditional cut crystal to clear tulip-shaped glasses.

Scotland's Glencairn Crystal developed the Glencairn whisky glass in 2001 and it is now widely used in the world's best whisky bars. This glass concentrates the aromas into a narrow space towards the lip of the glass, focusing the whisky experience in a very accurate way.

The renowned Austrian glass producer Georg Riedel designed the Vinum single malt glass in the mid-

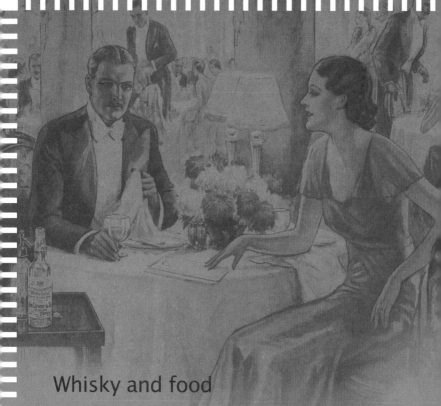

Whisky and food

Whisky can be a great accompaniment to food. Cheese, especially, goes well with whisky. Try pairing Highland Scotch whiskies with hard ewe's milk cheeses such as Manchego or Provolone; Bourbon with a rich, mature Gouda or even a mature cheddar; Canadian or American Rye – or even a big, smoky Islay – with a blue cheese such as Stilton, Lanark Blue or Rocquefort; Campbeltown with feta. Experimentation is part of the fun.

The art of matching food to whisky is making sure that the whisky does not swamp the flavours of the food – and vice versa. Macallan 12 Fine Oak is well matched with seared scallops and fettuccini; Glen Grant 16 Years Old with smoked salmon; BenRiach 16 Years Old Sauternes Finish is particularly delicious with a leg of lamb stuffed with fruit and spices; Glen Elgin 1975 works surprisingly well with a summer fruit salad; king prawns and an olive tapenade with Isle of Jura Superstition. The list is almost endless and only restricted by your imagination.

▲ A smart couple enjoy dinner and a whisky in a 1930s Dewar's advert.

1990s. This has a flared lip, which delivers the spirit to the front of the tongue, emphasizing the sweetness and creaminess of the first taste of the whisky.

Wilson and Morgan of Edinburgh produce a tasting glass for the connoisseur, designed for single malts, that is as fat as a Michelin man and features a petal rim, plus a hat for keeping in the aromas. The whisky in your glass has taken many years to reach such a pinnacle of perfection, so you shouldn't miss out on the full appreciation of it by serving it in a container that does not do it justice.

Measures

In whisky terms, many measures are somewhat indeterminate in exact quantity. In the UK, the old standard pub measures of anything from a sixth to a quarter of a gill (a gill is equal to a quarter of a pint, or 142 ml) were replaced in 1994 by multiples of 25 ml. Historically, the Scottish pint was larger than its English counterpart, the Scots variety being equal to one third of an imperial gallon, so that a Scots gill was always a good measure. A 'dram' in a public house can be any one of the measures listed above, but a 'dram' in a private home can be anything from a splash, which merely dampens the bottom of the glass, to great tumblers full of whisky. A 'glass' or 'gless' is normally accepted to be a double measure in a public house or a large dram in a private home.

2

Scotland
& the UK

Single malts

Scotland's Golden Triangle is the area into which is squeezed almost half of all Scotland's malt whisky distilleries. In the summer of 2010, there were 92 operating malt whisky distilleries in Scotland; of these, 47 are Speyside malts. Speyside's malts are the sweetest in Scotland, the peating levels are generally lower than other areas and sherry casks feature most frequently in the maturation process, a practice that enhances the richness of its whiskies.

Aberlour distillery

ABERLOUR, BANFFSHIRE, WWW.ABERLOUR.COM

Formerly called 'Charlestown of Aberlour', the village has now simplified its name to Aberlour. The distillery's water supply comes from St Drostan's well, so-named because the early Christian saint baptized converts with its waters.

Aberlour a'Bunadh

Bottled at cask strength and without chill-filtration, a process that standardizes the spirit, but can damage the flavours, a'Bunadh (which from the Gaelic, means 'original') has been matured exclusively in Oloroso Sherry casks. This sweetens the whisky and results in a big-bodied, mature and darkly nutty aroma of cooking apples and oranges, while the flavour is rich with citrus and cocoa-flavoured peat notes.

BenRiach distillery

NR. ELGIN, MORAY, WWW.BENRIACHDISTILLERY.CO.UK

The distillery was originally opened in 1898, just two years before the market crashed forcing it to close, and the distillery did not open again until 1965. Bought by private investors in 2004, the floor malting was in use until 1999, but could be reactivated. Their single malt has been restyled as the BenRiach.

The BenRiach 12 Years Old

Aromas of apples, flowering heather, honey and vanilla supported by a soft peat touch are followed by a silky, medium-sweet flavour of apple and peach, which finishes long, elegant and spicy with a note of milk chocolate.

▼ The BenRiach Speyside whisky distillery near Elgin, Scotland.

Benromach distillery

FORRES, MORAY, WWW.BENROMACH.COM

The distillery has had many owners in its time; it is now owned by Elgin Whisky Merchants, Gordon & MacPhail. Built in 1898 to a design by famed distillery architect, Charles Doig, the building has high-pitched gables and narrow, mullioned windows in the Scots vernacular style of the 17th century.

Benromach Traditional

Medium-bodied and medium-sweet with malty cereals, citrus and smoke, followed by a medium-sweet flavour of honey and spicy background peat, which has just a slight medicinal hint.

Glendullan distillery

DUFFTOWN, BANFFSHIRE

This was the last distillery to be built in Dufftown in the 19th century and prompted the epithet: 'Rome was built on seven hills, but Dufftown was built on seven stills.'

Glendullan 16 Years Old Centenary bottling

A classic and much under-rated whisky. With notes of new cut grass, ripe pineapple and peach, this is an elegant mouthful of crème brûlée, toffee, coffee and a delicate underlay of peat on the finish.

Glen Elgin distillery

LONGMORN, NR. ELGIN, MORAY

When this was built, it was the last distillery to be built in Speyside in the 19th century – and there was not another built in the area until 1958.

Glen Elgin 16 Years Old

A new bottling at cask strength of 58.5 per cent ABV, this has mature, decadent characters: a dark malty note with hazelnuts and toasted oak, honey, beeswax, tangerines and plums sitting on a bed of delicate peat and just a touch of dark chocolate on the tail.

Glenfarclas distillery

MARYPARK, BALLINDALLOCH, BANFFSHIRE,

WWW.GLENFARCLAS.CO.UK

Privately owned by the Grant family since 1836 and with the largest stills in Speyside, Glenfarclas has always produced outstanding whiskies. All of the distillery's output is now filled into sherry casks. You can buy bottles from every vintage stretching back to 1952 in a series known as the Family Casks.

Glenfarclas 21 Years Old

This is company chairman John Grant's favourite: aromas of orange marmalade, sweet vanilla, raisins, apples and a little mint mingle together, while the flavour is luscious and big-bodied with gently chewy tannins and plum, coffee and sweet toffee characters finishing with a softly smoky nuttiness.

Glenfarclas 40 Years Old

Possibly one of the finest commercially available whiskies. Rich and quite buttery with a little honey, clove and dried apricots supported by leather and good background peat, its flavour is medium-sweet, quite malty and mature with touches of chocolate, orange and spice, and the surprisingly fresh finish of malt, liquorice and sweet oak lasts forever.

Glenfiddich distillery

DUFFTOWN, BANFFSHIRE, WWW.GLENFIDDICH.COM

Makers of arguably the first widely available single
malt as the company was one of the first to actively
market their brand, and now the most successful
single malt. Demand for the whisky means that
the distillery's stillhouse now boasts no fewer than
28 stills. The distillery's visitor centre is the most
successful in the industry and attracts in excess of
125,000 visitors every year.

Glenfiddich 30 Years Old

Not the oldest 'Fiddich, but arguably the best value.
Sweet and showing beeswax, a sherry nuttiness,
creamy chocolate and just a suggestion of ginger on

▼ Barrels
welcoming
international
visitors at the
world-famous
Glenfiddich
distillery in
Dufftown,
Scotland.

the nose, the palate adds cocoa, juicy satsuma
oranges and pears and finishes with a flourish of
apples, coffee and dark chocolate.

Glen Grant distillery

ROTHES, MORAY, WWW.GLENGRANT.COM

Glen Grant distillery dates back to 1840 and,
unusually, all the stills are direct fired. To the rear
of the distillery is an award-winning garden and,
hidden in a safe built into the rock at the top of the
garden, there is a secret supply of whisky to refresh
you after your climb up the path.

Glen Grant 16 Years Old

Full-bodied, quite austere with fruity apples and
apricots supported by soft oaky vanilla and a delicate
touch of smokiness, finishing firm and rich with
honey and toffee apples.

The Glenlivet distillery

BALINDALLOCH, BANFFSHIRE, WWW.THEGLENLIVET.COM

As a result of Royal patronage in 1821, Glenlivet
whisky attained a cult status and resulted in the
name being appended to many distilleries. This, the
original, has adopted the definitive article to separate
its from its imitators.

The Glenlivet Archive 21 Years Old

Citrus, honey and mature characters such as
marmalade, apricots, raisins and coconut are to the
fore with beeswax, gently chewy oak tannins,
butterscotch and ginger on the palate; this finishes
gloriously complex and surprisingly fresh.

Glenrothes distillery

ROTHES, MORAY, WWW.THEGLENROTHES.COM

The distillery pioneered the use of vintages instead of an age statement on its labels and you will find the difference between a hot vintage like 1993 and a cooler one like 1998 very enlightening.

The Glenrothes 1998

Medium-bodied and sherried with nuts, beeswax, cinnamon, creamy hazelnuts and smoky tangerines; the flavour is round, smooth, creamy, medium-sweet and rich with dark orange and apricot notes finishing long, softly tangy with a coffee and fruitcake character and quite zesty citrus on the tail.

The Glenrothes 1994

Quite full-bodied and fresh, some coffee, vanilla and honey; with water bringing out cloves, liquorice, pears and ripe peaches, while the palate is rich, nutty and medium-sweet with a little touch of spice, some honey and tangy vanilla; finishing elegant and fresh with butterscotch and rich lemon curd.

Linkwood distillery

ELGIN, MORAY

There is a belief amongst distillers that nothing about a distillery should be changed in case it changes the character of the spirit. Roderick Mackenzie, who was manager here from 1945 to 1963 didn't even allow the removal of spiders' webs. Despite this, Linkwood, which was originally built in 1821, has been totally rebuilt three times as demand has grown for its make.

Linkwood 12 Years Old

Beautifully apple-scented with some blossom and a soft smokiness at the back; lemon zest plays across the top aroma notes and the flavour is medium-sweet and rounded with apple to the fore and a little smoke, finishing elegantly with some spice and lingering sweetness.

Longmorn distillery

NR. ELGIN, MORAY

Another distillery whose make is under-rated by drinkers but valued as top dressing by blenders. The name comes from the Gaelic 'Llanmorgund', which translates as 'place of the holy man', as the distillery was built on the site of an ancient church.

Longmorn 16 Years Old

Rich and full-bodied with a cooked apples/grapey fruitiness underlaid by sweet coconut and a hint of pepper, this is medium-sweet and round with flavours of marzipan biscuit, gentle tannins and a delicate edge of peat. The finish is rich and elegant with a light hint of smokiness.

Macallan distillery

CRAIGELLACHIE, MORAY, WWW.THEMACALLAN.COM

Probably the most collected of all malts, there are now quite a formidable range of ages and vintages available in bottle. Established at Easter Elchies farm, close to a fording point on the River Spey, the whisky distilled at the old farm distillery was a popular bonus for the drovers moving their cattle to market. The whisky is known as 'The Macallan' and much of the make is aged in sherry casks.

The Macallan Sherry Oak 12 Years Old
Quite a step up from the 10 Years Old, this has an intensely fruity nose, with peach, apple, banana, black cherry, raspberry and blackcurrant vying with cinnamon for the top spot. The flavour is more dried fruits – apricots, raisins and dates in an iced cake – finishing long, rich and elegant with some cloves coming to the surface.

Speyside distillery
KINGUSSIE, INVERNESS-SHIRE,
WWW.SPEYSIDEDISTILLERY.CO.UK

To the east of Kingussie is this relatively new distillery which was founded in 1962 by George Christie but had a 34-year gestation period before the spirit first ran on 12 December 1990. The distillery has two pot stills of traditional shape, but since large-scale production was never an aim of Christie's, they are some of the smallest in Scotland.

Speyside 12 Years Old
Quite big-bodied with slightly perfumed dark peat and chocolate notes tinged with medicinal aniseed. The flavour is round and smooth with some beeswax, tar and toffee, which finishes with a surprisingly delicate peat note.

The Highlands

The Highland whiskies are drier than Speysides and have more body than those from the Lowlands.

Aberfeldy distillery
ABERFELDY, PERTHSHIRE

The distillery building has a definite Presbyterian architectural appearance. Owned by Dewar's and adding its own impact to that blend, the distillery visitor centre, Dewar's World of Whisky, has won many awards.

Aberfeldy 18 Years Old

Full-bodied, with waxy notes of heather honey, ripe, mature orange marmalade, lanolin, liquorice and a floral touch; the flavour is sweet, of good body with quite soft peat notes and citrus, ripe orange/lemon and creamy vanilla, finishing long, very clean, impressive and ethereal with a note of dry tannin on the end.

Ardmore distillery
KENNETHMONT, ABERDEENSHIRE,
WWW.ARDMOREWHISKY.COM

The distillery's make is a key ingredient in the Teacher's Highland Cream blend. Despite many innovations, the stills remained coal-fired until 2001 when, after a major fire in the stillhouse, they switched to indirect steam heating.

The morning dram

Whisky has been credited with medicinal properties and, while that claim is regularly disputed, its benefit as personal central heating has been enjoyed for centuries. Dr Samuel Johnson, in his *A Journey to the Western Isles of Scotland* (1775), recorded 'A man of the Hebrides, as soon as he appears in the morning, swallows a glass of whisky; yet they are not a drunken race, at least I never was present at much intemperance; but no man is so abstemious as to refuse the morning dram, which they call a "skalk".' Skalk is the anglicization of the Gaelic world 'Scailg'. Unfortunately, this habit of the morning dram has all but died out.

Ardmore Traditional

Double matured – firstly in bourbon casks and then finished off in small quarter casks that allow more oak influence. Quite full-bodied and obviously peaty with some creaminess and buttery vanilla backed up by banana, citrus and a little coconut; the flavour is quite sweet, which you might find jars a little with the earthy peat note; it finishes long with a dark peat note and some butterscotch-coated lemon zest.

Balblair distillery

EDDERTON, ROSS-SHIRE, WWW.BALBLAIR.COM

The local area was historically so famous for illicit stills that it has long been known as 'The Parish of Peats'. There are records of brewing of ale on the site from 1749, although the present distillery was built in 1872.

Balblair 1989

Medium-sweet, very fresh and quite full-bodied, this has peach and apple fruit notes with soft, round, toffee vanilla and delicate peat, which resurrects as tarry rope in the dark and tangy finish.

Ben Nevis distillery

LOCHY BRIDGE, FORT WILLIAM, INVERNESS-SHIRE
WWW.BENNEVISDISTILLERY.COM

Situated at the base of, and taking its name from, Scotland's highest mountain, the distillery was founded by 'Long John' MacDonald in 1825. It was acquired by Japanese company Nikka in 1989.

Ben Nevis 1975 26 Years Old

Quite full-bodied and complex with burnt, treacly toffee, Olde English marmalade oranges, oily, oaky vanilla and quite a solid peat note; the flavour is full, fruity, chocolate-coated orange and smoky Turkish Delight; finishing long with a dark chocolate note, very elegant, lingering and complex.

▲ Ardmore distillery, nestled in a picturesque valley in Kennethmont, Scotland.

Clynelish distillery

BRORA, SUTHERLAND

The current distillery was built in 1967 next to the original Clynelish, which was established in 1819. The original distillery was set up to utilize the barley grown on the coastal strip by farmers who had been cleared off their crofts inland to make way for sheep.

Clynelish 14 Years Old

Quite big-bodied with a citrus fruitiness, a soft malty touch, demerara sugar-coated soft, sweet oak and chocolate and cocoa; the flavour is of ripe hazelnuts in creamy vanilla with a dark, oaty peat note;

finishing long and elegant with a touch of bitter whole-nut chocolate and tinged with seaweed.

Dalmore distillery

ALNESS, ROSS-SHIRE, WWW.THEDALMORE.COM

Situated on a very picturesque site on the shores of the Cromarty Firth, Dalmore was established in 1839 by Alexander Matheson. The top half of each spirit still is surrounded by a copper tulip-shaped cooling jacket, which serves as an additional condenser, ensuring that only the finest alcohols are permitted into the final spirit.

Dalmore 12 Years Old

Fresh, clean and medium-dry with good richness, soft vanilla and grapey mandarin orange scents; the flavour has a solid, masculine note supported by elegantly knit peat. The finish is almost dry, lightly malty and very distinguished.

Dalmore 40 Years Old

A whisky that is big and dark, exhibiting muscovado sugar, medicinal tar and honey with mature Olde English marmalade, tangerines and delicate peat; the flavour is big, round, medium-sweet and velvety smooth with spice tingling across your tongue and a very gentle chewy toffee note; finishing very long, elegant and ethereal with a soft peat note.

Edradour distillery

PITLOCHRY, PERTHSHIRE, WWW.EDRADOUR.COM

Edradour is the smallest distillery in Scotland, whose output is only enough spirit to fill 12 casks every week. It returned to independent ownership in 2002, when it was taken over by Signatory Vintage Malt Whisky Co. Ltd.

Edradour Supertuscan Finish

Medium-bodied, grappa-like and slightly unctuous with notes of chocolate-dipped cherries, forest fruits and olives; the flavour is medium-sweet and very complex with vanilla custard, dark fruit, chocolate and spice tingling across the tongue, and then finishing with a flavour of delicate strawberry fruit and a little floral note.

Glendronach distillery

FORGUE, BY HUNTLY, ABERDEENSHIRE,
WWW.GLENDRONACHDISTILLERY.CO.UK

A variety of owners over the years have developed the distillery. Since 1960, it has been an ingredient in the Teacher's Highland Cream blend. Its make has long been a favourite among whisky aficionados.

The Glendronach Revival 15 Years Old

A gentle giant of a whisky, which terrifies initially and then shows its compassionate centre: quite big-bodied with some candle wax and dried fruit – almost burnt fruit cake, some charred oak, some stewed apples and a little diesel note; the flavour is full-bodied with a dark peat note, gently chewy with characters of Brazil nuts; finishing very long, powerful and really quite elegant and complex with soft, malty fruit on the tail.

Glenglassaugh distillery

NR. PORTSOY, ABERDEENSHIRE
WWW.GLENGLASSAUGH.COM

Despite the fact that Glenglassaugh had been open for less than 10 years when Alfred Barnard, a British brewing and distilling historian, visited in 1885, he described its make as: 'steadily gaining favour in the market' and, despite years of closure inbetween, it continues to be held in high esteem.

Glenglassaugh 26 Years Old

Rich, sherry complexity with buttery vanilla shortbread notes dipped in strawberries and creamy toffee; the flavour is medium-dry and nutty with liquorice, almonds and dried fruits; finishing fresh, slightly minty and sherried.

Glengoyne distillery

DUMGOYNE, KILLEARN, STIRLINGSHIRE
WWW.GLENGOYNE.COM

Nestling under Dumgoyne Hill, the distillery has remained fiercely independent during its 177 years. Its warehouses are south of the Highland Line, which passes the distillery on the highland side.

Glengoyne 40 Years Old

Medium-bodied, with some green aromas, demerara sugar and red-skinned apples, spice notes of nutmeg, fennel and dark, nutty toffee; the flavour is medium-dry, with soft, rich toffee, good body and a cereal note. It has a smooth, oily vanilla character, with some honeycomb and finishes very long and clean with some cardamom and a note of grapefruit.

Glenmorangie distillery

TAIN, ROSS-SHIRE, WWW.GLENMORANGIE.COM

One of the leading malts around the world, it has the tallest stills in Scotland at 5.14 metres. The height of the stills means that only the finest and most delicate of flavours fall over the lyne arm. As of spring, 2009, the number of stills increased to 12.

Glenmorangie 25 Years Old

Quite big-bodied and pungent, intense, musky and perfumed with a homemade blackcurrant jam aroma backed up by sandalwood, vanilla, some spice and a hint of dark chocolate; the flavour is quite big-bodied, with notes of cocoa and chocolate, spice and luscious ripe orange; finishing round and with a note of creamy macchiato, some dried orange peel and yet retaining a mouth-watering zingy, citrus zestiness.

Old Pulteney distillery

WICK, CAITHNESS, WWW.OLDPULTENEY.COM

The most northerly distillery on the UK mainland and named after Pulteneytown, the district of the town of Wick in which the distillery was built. Wick was built on the fishing industry, but it is distilling that has survived as the fishing industry became a pale shadow of what it once was. The distillery's wash stills are truncated, with the lyne arms coming off below the top of the stills. When the stills were delivered, it was discovered that they were too tall for the stillhouse, so the tops were cut off. The result is that the heavier alcohols do not fall over the lyne arm making the spirit more elegant.

Old Pulteney 17 Years Old

Medium-bodied, slightly vegetal and nutty with notes of coconut and pineapple supported by tarry rope and a soft sea influence; the flavour is medium-dry, of good weight, rich, soft and easy with a touch of spice and some malty honey; finishing long and elegant with liquorice, pine needles and salty lips.

Tullibardine distillery

BLACKFORD, PERTHSHIRE, WWW.TULLIBARDINE.COM

The work of the leading distillery designer, William Delme-Evans and built in 1949, the buildings of this distillery had lain mothballed for 10 years when they were bought by a quartet of businessmen who have developed the site as an essential tourist destination. The area is known for the quality of its water: a brewery on the site was awarded a Royal Charter following a visit from King James IV in 1488 and there are two mineral water companies based within 5 miles of the distillery.

Tullibardine 1993

Fresh and malty with a peppery peat note, an edge of sweetness and a green, hedgerow character; the flavour is medium-dry with good body and a character of creamy hazelnut caramels; finishing long, rich and elegant with the malt springing up again on the tail.

The Keepers of the Quaich

In 1988, the Keepers of the Quaich was formed at Blair Castle in Perthshire, founded by a group of competing distilling companies to promote Scotch whisky and encourage other companies within the industry. A Quaich is a communal drinking bowl that originated in 17th-century Edinburgh and Glasgow. The society's Quaich is 61 cm in diameter and was created by Graham Stewart, a silversmith from Dunblane. Membership is by invitation only and the Keepers are individuals who have made some significant contribution to the industry. Their motto reads '*Uisge beatha Gu Brath*' which, translated from the Gaelic means 'Whisky For Ever'!

The Lowlands

Lowland whiskies are the lightest and driest of Scotland's output and are located in an area south of a line drawn between Cardross in the west and Dundee in the east.

Auchentoshan distillery

DALMUIR, CLYDEBANK, DUNBARTONSHIRE,

WWW.AUCHENTOSHAN.COM

Triple-distilled and unpeated, Auchentoshan's name is derived from the Gaelic for 'corner of the field'.

Auchentoshan 12 Years Old

Fresh and clean with floral and toasty toffee notes; the flavours are dry and rich with citrus and peach; finishing with a touch of cereal.

Bladnoch distillery

BLADNOCH, WIGTOWN, DUMFRIES & GALLOWAY,

WWW.BLADNOCH.COM

Bladnoch is the most southerly distillery in Scotland and home to the Whisky School, where visitors can get hands-on experience making whisky.

Bladnoch 8 Years Old

A fresh lunchtime malt, full of life, medium-bodied and malty, showing lemons and grapefruit, a slight medicinal note, some cereal, hazelnut and toffee; the flavours are medium-dry and rich with an oily, vanilla smoothness; finishing soft and languorous.

Isle of Islay

Islay's whiskies are the most peat- and sea-influenced of all Scotland's malts. The smoky character is one you either love or hate. The island is only 14 miles long and 8 miles wide and the ocean weather washes over the island, greatly influencing its whiskies.

Ardbeg distillery

NEAR PORT ELLEN, ISLE OF ISLAY, WWW.ARDBEG.COM

Ardbeg's make is the most heavily peated of all Scotland's whiskies at 50 parts per million. It has always been a favourite of Islay aficionados, but was closed more often than open in the 30 years prior to being taken over by Glenmorangie in 1997.

Ardbeg Corryvreckan

Everything that the 10 Years Old has, but in spades: tar, chocolate and burnt mahogany, notes of shellfish, citrus backed up by sandalwood; the flavour is dry, big-bodied and intensely smoky; finishing long and explosive with huge peat notes and lemon and lime on the tail.

Bowmore distillery

BOWMORE, ISLE OF ISLAY, WWW.BOWMORE.COM

The distillery stands fortress-like, alongside the harbour in the town of Bowmore. The distillery gave a warehouse to the town and it was converted into a swimming pool heated by the waste heat from the distillery. The various bottlings from the company have proved very collectable in recent years.

▲ A wooden bung in a barrel at Ardbeg distillery, Isle of Islay, Scotland.

Bowmore 18 Years Old

Quite full with damp autumn leaves and chestnuts, charred stick peat and violets; with water, heather opens up with some green appleskins, caramel, tobacco and seaweed. It has good body and the flavour is round and sherried with liquorice, floral and chocolate with a carbolic note; finishing long with a sense of sweetness, quite rich and with a burnt chocolate note on the tail.

Bruichladdich distillery

BRUICHLADDICH, ISLE OF ISLAY,
WWW.BRUICHLADDICH.COM

The lightest and most delicate of Islay's whiskies. In 1995 the distillery was closed, but a consortium of 25 private investors took it over in 2001. Since then there has been a mind-boggling array of bottlings. Affectionately known as 'Laddie', Bruichladdich is pronounced 'Brew-ich-laddie'.

Bruichladdich 15 Years Old

Medium-bodied with a touch of nuttiness. The flavour is round, smooth, medium-dry with softly chewy tannins and gently peated; finishing quite ethereal and elegant with a touch of perfume.

Caol Ila distillery

PORT ASKAIG, ISLE OF ISLAY

On the east coast, just to the north of Port Askaig, the stillhouse has the finest view of any distillery, across to the Paps of Jura. Sea water is used in condensing the evaporate from Caol Ila's stills. Caol Ila is pronounced 'Kaal-eela'.

▲ Inside a still at Bowmore, the oldest working distillery on Islay.

Malting and fermentation

Bowmore distillery adds an extra layer of flavour to its whisky by turning to tradition. In exactly the same manner of a farmer of 500 years ago, Bowmore's barley is soaked in the peat-stained waters of the River Laggan and laid out onto its malting floor, encouraging the seeds to germinate. During germination, the starch inside the seed is converted to fermentable sugars. The grain is then heated over a peat-fed open fire whose heat stops the germination so that, while some of the fermentable sugars have been used to

fuel growth, there remains a considerable amount within the seed's shell. Once dried, the green malt is ground into a coarse flour known as 'grist'. To this, hot water is added, giving a hot, sweet, sticky liquid called 'wort'. Yeast is added to the wort and bacterial fermentation converts the sugar to alcohol, resulting in a high alcohol beer known as 'wash'.

Caol Ila 18 Years Old

Big-bodied and powerful with a classic Caol Ila nose of burnt heather roots complemented by soft oaky vanilla. There is also a touch of antiseptic and some citrus. The flavour is dry and powerful, rich, smooth and charred with a slight edge of sweetness, which finishes with notes of tar and chocolate, dry smoke and melon.

Laphroaig distillery

NR. PORT ELLEN, ISLE OF ISLAY, WWW.LAPHROAIG.COM

Situated on the south coast of Islay and facing the prevailing south-westerly weather, Laphroaig's annual storm damage bill is considerable; in high winds, the seaweed is piled up against the distillery walls and can often be found hanging from the roof. This is why Laphroaig's make is so sea-tainted.

Laphroaig 18 Years Old

Quite soft for Laphroaig, honey, creamy toffee apples and pepper supported by sooty peat smoke and some tar with seaweed, iodine and ginger. The flavour is big-bodied, dry and of peat smoke with a sweetness, tarry oranges and honeyed seaweed; finishing spicy with sweetly toasted oak and a bonfire on the beach.

Campbeltown

In the early 20th century, Campbeltown was known as the 'whisky capital' of Scotland because of the number of distilleries – at one point, there were 32 in production. Over-production during Prohibition in the USA led to a reduction in quality and consumers lost faith in Campbeltown's whiskies. By 1935, all the distilleries had closed. Since then, only three have reopened, Glen Scotia, Glengyle and Springbank.

Springbank distillery

LONGROW, CAMPBELTOWN, ARGYLL,
WWW.SPRINGBANKWHISKY.COM

The team at Springbank could be called 'eccentric': they do things their way. It has been run by members of the same family for 173 years. Everything, from malting through to bottling and despatch is carried out at this site. Although the stillhouse has three stills, it is not triple-distilled, it is distilled two and a half times. Longrow (heavily peated) and Hazelburn (triple-distilled) are also produced at Springbank.

Springbank 18 Years Old

Of medium weight with rich, oily oak and marzipan, quite a lot of red fruit – strawberries and raspberries – supported by liquorice and dark honey and treacle toffee; the flavour has dried fruits: apricots, raisins, pineapple and coconut; finishing with great length, some smoky oak, dark chocolate, a little tarry rope, liquorice and Springbank's classic salty lips.

Other Islands

Highland Park distillery

HOLM ROAD, KIRKWALL, ORKNEY

Scotland's most northerly distillery is located on Orkney's Mainland. Twenty per cent of the distillery's malt requirements are still produced from its malting floor. Orkney's cool climatic conditions – the average temperature in winter is 6°C and 15°C in summer – mean that the whisky matures slowly and evenly.

Highland Park 40 Years Old
Quite full-bodied and mature with notes of orange, vanilla and honey – soft, buttery and creamy with notes of hazelnut, brioche and popcorn. The flavour is medium-dry, round and rich, a touch of spice tingles across the tongue; there are hints of orange, walnuts and pistachios, buttered wholemeal bread and it is smooth and creamy. The finish has a long and ethereal centre with rich edges, a little tangy note and some salt appears on the tail.

Isle of Arran distillery

LOCHRANZA, ISLE OF ARRAN, WWW.ARRANWHISKY.COM

Legal distilling was re-established on the island of Arran after 150 years. The modern distillery is traditional in its outlook, but blends easily within the surrounding landscape. Golden eagles inhabit the hills above the distillery and are a frequent feature of the distillery's open days.

Arran Rowan Tree

A more delicate style, with floral, toffee, biscuity and lavender notes, a hint of coffee and some citrus – orange and lime; the flavour is drier than the core malts, clean, rich and smooth with a wee touch of spice, and some chocolate-topped cappuccino; finishing long, clean, fresh and quite ethereal with a touch of espresso and a lavender floral note.

▲ A red-hot peat-fire kiln at Highland Park distillery, Orkney, Scotland.

Isle of Jura distillery

CRAIGHOUSE, ISLE OF JURA, WWW.JURAWHISKY.COM

As the crow flies, Craighouse is 66 miles from the company's head office in Glasgow, but the journey takes almost a whole day, covers 130 miles by road and includes two ferry trips.

Jura Superstition

Big-bodied with a dried fruit note, rich nuttiness, toffee, marzipan, heather honey and lots of earthy peat; the flavour is quite big-bodied, medium-dry, but very rich and smooth with honey and a creaminess supported by peat. The finish is long, complex and impressively rich with a sweet edge, some liquorice and tideline notes with a touch of pine needles.

Blends

The blending of heavily flavoured malts with more refined grain whiskies produces a more easy-drinking whisky with some elegance.

Black Bull 12 Years Old (Duncan Taylor & Co.)
Weighty, chocolate-coated, sherried green apples and peaches with delicate peat; smooth and elegant.

Black Bottle (Burn Stewart)
Superbly blended, of good weight with burnt heather and chocolate with sea notes and a hint of sweetness.

Chivas Regal 12 Years Old (Pernod Ricard)
Smooth and sweet, honeyed, fruity and gently nutty; a great blend with complex undertones.

Cutty Sark (Edrington)
Fresh and honeyed with vanilla oak and orange/citrus – a wonderful lunchtime drink.

Dewar's (Bacardi)
Honey, vanilla, soft peat smoke and toffee with a firm note of malt; wonderful balance, elegant and easy.

Monkey Shoulder (William Grant)
A blend of three Speyside malts, quite full-bodied, grapefruit and pineapple flavoured with spice, chocolate and toffee.

England and Wales

Although England and Wales are not as well known for their whisky production as their Scottish and Irish neighbours, there are still a few distilleries that are worth seeking out.

St George's distillery

ROUDHAM, NORFOLK, WWW.ENGLISHWHISKY.CO.UK

A farming family with 600 years history of growing and processing grain, the Nelstrops opened their distillery late in 2006 on land down by the River Thet. They pulled in Iain Henderson, who had just retired after 30 years distilling in Scotland, to oversee the spirit production.

St George's Chapter 9

Medium-bodied with a smoky, charred oak note; water brings out the sweetness and delicate lime and apricot fruit; the flavour is medium-dry, with the sweetness growing, of good weight with rich vanilla and finishing cleanly and quite complex with smoky spices and chocolate.

Penderyn distillery

PENDERYN, WALES, WWW.WELSH-WHISKY.CO.UK

Penderyn is the first distillery operational in Wales since the late 19th century and is located in the heart of the Brecon Beacons National Park. It uses a unique form of still that is very energy efficient; it has a

traditional pot beneath a tall rectifying column. Their wash is supplied by Welsh brewer, S A Brain & Co.

Penderyn Welsh Whisky Sherrywood
Fresh, clean and unpeated with slight floral and rich, quite dark fruit notes, a little pepper, toffee, beeswax and green apple skins. The flavour is medium-dry with an edge of sweetness and clean with a touch of spice tingling across the tongue; finishing creamy with caramel, ginger and honey notes.

The Independents

The independent bottlers grew out of the whisky broking side of the whisky industry and have predominantly originated in Scotland. An independent bottler is a business that buys casks of whisky, either as newly filled casks that must be laid down to mature, or else as a part of an unrequired parcel of casks. The independent bottler will then have the contents of these casks filled into bottles when they consider the whisky to be ready.

Many of these companies are relatively small, family-owned businesses; many of their bottlings are of single casks, yielding a small number of bottles and, therefore, are very close to unrepeatable as each cask imposes a slightly different thumbprint to the whisky inside it. Most of the independents interfere with the whisky as little as possible, so very few nowadays add E51, the caramel colouring used in many commercial bottlings, and few chill-filter.

A commercial bottler may bottle between 100 and 200 casks of their 12 Years Old whisky, this averages out the flavour characteristics of the individual cask, allowing the distiller to make a flavour statement and impose a signature, which can be very closely replicated in the next bottling. The independent bottler, because of the small number of bottles involved is interacting with the more informed consumer who appreciates the uniqueness of the single cask.

Berry Brothers & Rudd

3 ST JAMES STREET, LONDON, W6 9RW, WWW.BBR.COM

The company, originally established in 1698, now owns The Glenrothes brand and holds a Royal Warrant to supply alcoholic beverages to the Queen. They have bottled whiskies under their own 'Berry's Own Selection' label for over 100 years.

▲ Berry Bros. & Rudd, established in 1698, fine wine and spirits merchants with a broking exchange, wine tasting events and schools.

Wm Cadenhead

83 LONGROW, CAMPBELTOWN, ARGYLL, PA28 6EX, WWW.WMCADENHEAD.COM

Scotland's oldest firm of independent bottlers and therefore at the forefront of single malt marketing.

They have stores in Edinburgh, London and Campbeltown and franchises across Europe.

Cárn Mòr

MORRISON AND MACKAY WHISKY, HILTON, PERTHSHIRE, PH1 4EB, WWW.MANDMWHISKY.CO.UK

The new boy on the block, and a tourist destination, the centre bottled their first casks in 2007, but the management's previous whisky expertise means that this now forms an important part of the business.

Compass Box Whisky Co.

9 POWER ROAD, LONDON, W4 5YN
WWW.COMPASSBOXWHISKY.COM

This company, founded by John Glaser, produces innovative and imaginative bottlings. Glaser has been referred to as the Scotch whisky industry's *bête noire* because of his attempts to drag them into the 21st century. He doesn't believe in age statements, but bottles when he considers the whiskies to be ready.

▲ Whisky innovators Compass Box Whisky Co. released the Lost Blend Limited Edition, 2014.

A. Dewar Rattray Ltd

32 MAIN ROAD, KIRKOSWALD, AYRSHIRE, KA19 8HY, WWW.DEWARRATTRAY.COM

Founded in 1868 as an importer of French wines, Italian spirits and olive oil, the business was returned to the family of one of its founders in 2004 when it was bought by Tim Morrison. They now specialize in single malt whiskies and their own label, Stronachie.

Cask characteristics

Whisky barrels are made by hand from oak and the thickness of the staves will vary from cask to cask. Therefore no cooper or distiller will guarantee the exact quantity contained within a cask.

The staves are curved by the application of flame, which softens the cellulose in the wood and allows it to be bent. Sherry casks are toasted on the inside, which allows more of the wood tannins to flavour the whisky, while bourbon casks are charred, caramelizing the cellulose to give the spirit a sweet, vanilla note.

SINGLE CASK SCOTCH MALT WHISKY	
DATE DISTILLED	Apr 80
DATE BOTTLED	Sept 97
AGED IN OAK	17 yrs
PROOF STRENGTH	95.2° 54.4% vol e
CONTENTS BY VOL	70 cl

▲ Bottles from
the Scotch Malt
Whisky Society
are individually
coded.

The Scotch Malt Whisky Society

**THE VAULTS, 7 GILES STREET, EDINBURGH, EH6 6BZ, WWW.
SMWS.CO.UK**

This Edinburgh-based society bottles cask-strength
whiskies for its members. Each cask is bottled under
a numerical code, so as not to identify the source
distillery on the label. The Society now has branches
in Australia, Austria, France, Germany, Italy, Japan,
the Netherlands, South Africa, Sweden, Switzerland,
Taiwan and the USA.

Speyside Distillers Co. Ltd.

DUCHESS ROAD, RUTHERGLEN, GLASGOW, G73 1AU,

WWW.SPEYSIDEDISTILLERY.CO.UK

A brand name used by owners of Speyside distillery for a selection of single malt whiskies, originally selected by Robert Scott, their former distiller.

The Signatory Vintage Malt Whisky Company

EDRADOUR DISTILLERY, PITLOCHRY, PERTHSHIRE,

PH16 5JP, WWW.EDRADOUR.CO.UK

Established by Andrew Symington in Leith in 1988, Signatory bought Edradour distillery in 2002 and is now located there with an added a bottling hall.

The Vintage Malt Whisky Company

2 STEWART STREET, MILNGAVIE, GLASGOW, G62 6BW,

WWW.VINTAGEMALTWHISKY.COM

Set up by Brian Crook in 1992, the company bottles its single malt selections under the 'Cooper's Choice' label and also owns the brands Finlaggan, Tantallan and Glen Almond.

Wilson & Morgan

24 GREAT KING STREET, EDINBURGH, EH3 6QN,

WWW.WILSONANDMORGAN.COM

Established by the Rossi family from Italy in 1992. The family had imported Scotch whisky into Italy for many years before setting up their own series of labels for mature bottling.

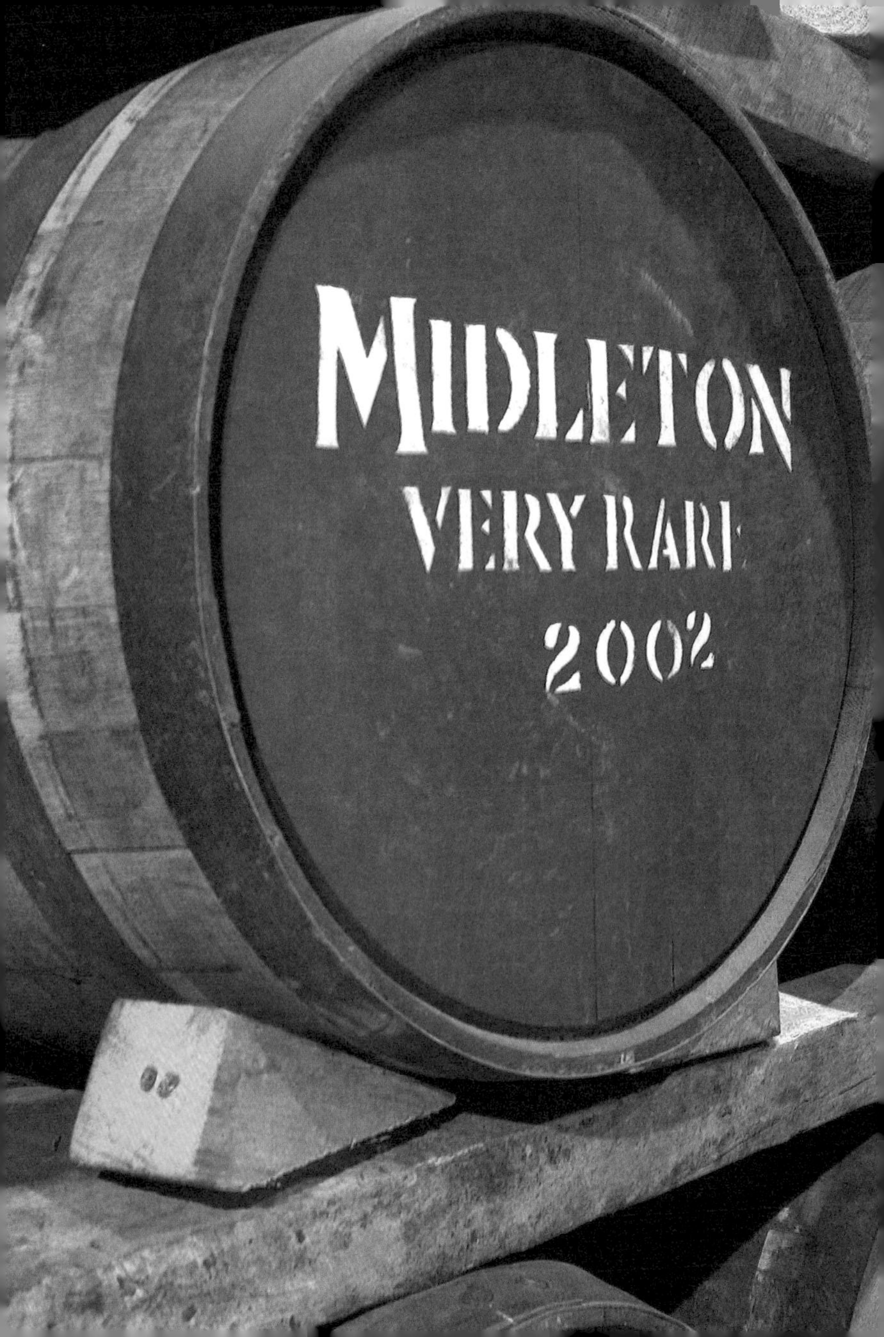
MIDLETON
VERY RARE
2002

3

Ireland

Irish distilleries

The Irish were arguably the first people to make whiskey. Its origins can be traced back to the 6th century. Sir Walter Raleigh is known to have dropped by to pick up a cask of Irish whiskey from Cork in 1595 en route to Guyana.

Scotch and Irish whiskey

The main difference between Scotch and Irish whiskey is that the latter is lighter because the Irish use a large portion of unmalted barley in their pot still production. Also, the malt for Scotch is dried over an open peat fire, which means the smoke that permeates the grains carries through to the final whisky. By contrast, in Ireland, the malt is dried in closed kilns using only hot air, not smoke. Few Irish whiskeys in recent years have used peat for the drying of their green malt, as they have had plentiful supplies of coal. By installing a number of different still shapes and sizes, the Irish have produced a wide variety of flavour within the same distillery.

The art of the distiller is to separate and retain the good elements of the alcohol family – the ones that, when mature, will make a good whiskey – and to separate and discard the undesirable elements – the ones that will simply give a hangover. In Ireland, this is done by distilling three times. The triple distillation produces a more refined, less characterful spirit than double distillation.

Diminishing distilleries

It is estimated that at the start of the 18th century there were around 2,000 distilleries in Ireland, but when the Irish Distillers Group was formed in 1966, there were only five distilleries left in production. Shortly afterwards, Jameson & Powers in Dublin, Tullamore and Cork distilleries ceased distilling. This reduced Ireland's distilleries to two: Bushmills in the north and the 'new' Midleton in the south. Since then, Cooley's has opened up and there is currently talk of a distillery being developed on the Dingle Peninsula in the south west.

▲ A tin plate advertising Jameson Irish whiskey.

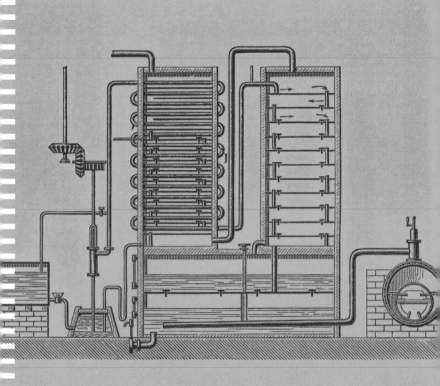

The column still

When Aeneas Coffey filed his patent for his column still in 1830, he was the proprietor of the Dock distillery in Dublin, which may have been why he was unable to get any of his fellow Irish distillers to use his newly invented still. They insisted on sticking with their pot stills which were more expensive to run and produced a more characterful spirit. Instead, he went to Scotland where he was welcomed with open arms by the Steins and Haigs who adopted the column still and developed grain whisky and, in the fullness of time, allowed the development of blended whisky.

Pure Pot Still

Pure (or 'single') pot still is the only style of whiskey that is exclusively made in Ireland. Where single malt is produced from 100 per cent malted barley, pure pot still whiskey uses a mix of malted and unmalted barley.

Old Bushmills distillery

BUSHMILLS, COUNTY ANTRIM, NORTHERN IRELAND, WWW.BUSHMILLS.COM

The world's original licensed distillery, with an original license date of 1608, although there are records of distillation in the area as far back as 1276. The stillhouse contains 10 stills, which are able to conjure up a wide variety of whiskey flavours.

Bushmills 16 Years Old

Full-bodied, fresh and slightly green with a gooseberry character. It has a rich, woody nuttiness and is medium-sweet with a toffee character; the flavour is almost dry with good body, smooth, dark; finishing with a good richness, a dark complexity and an almost mahogany-flavoured chewiness.

Cooley distillery

RIVERSTOWN, DUNDALK, COUNTY LOUTH, IRELAND

Cooley's was established in 1989 with one still just south of the border with the North. The company's creation broke the dominance of the industry by Irish Distillers and its presence enlivened the category.

Fiercely independent and innovative, they have reintroduced peat flavours into Irish whiskey with their Connemara brand.

Tyrconnel
Fresh and clean with a touch of liquorice, a good, ripe richness, medium-sweet and quite round with a slight unctuous character; the flavour is medium-sweet, fresh and smooth with good body; finishing clean with honey and an almost barley sugar sweetness and a slight citrus note.

Connemara
Quite full-bodied, fresh and medium-dry with a round fruitiness and a good measure of slightly green peatiness; the flavour is medium-sweet, with good body, a nice weight of peat and a round, dark nuttiness and it finishes long and clean with a background smokiness.

Greenore Single Grain
Light, delicate, fresh with sweet bourbon oaky vanilla notes and peaches; the flavour is rich and soft, quite mouth-watering with an oily oak/barley sugar character, which finishes fresh, clean and crisp.

Jameson Midleton distillery
MIDLETON, COUNTY CORK, IRELAND

Built alongside the original Midleton distillery, which now forms the distillery's visitor centre, in 1975, the new distillery is hidden from the public's eyes and yet produces most of the Irish whiskeys you will see on bar gantries around the world. It has three column

stills as well as nine very large pots. Outside the visitor centre is the world's largest pot still (31,648 gallons or 143,874 litres), which used to be worked inside the old distillery and is so large that they had to install it and build the distillery around it before supporting it from the roof to stop it imploding.

Midleton Very Rare 2010
Medium-bodied, lemon-scented with notes of honey, malt, charred mahogany, tea, zesty grapefruit and blackcurrant; the flavours are balanced, rich and dry with a touch of spice, some mint and some nutty toffee. The finish is long, complex and sweet with syrup and menthol occurring.

▲ An old delivery truck laden with whiskey barrels on display outside the Jameson Old Distillery at Midleton in County Cork, Ireland.

77

Barley beginnings

Among the factors that allows a distillery to produce a unique spirit is the mix of cereals used at the brewing stage of the process, in particular the ratio of malted barley to unmalted barley.

Unmalted barley was originally used because the Malt Act of 1725 taxed malted barley. These days each of the Irish Distillers' brands has a different mix of malted and unmalted barley and this mix contributes to the final flavour of each whiskey.

There is a traditional test used to determine the best barley, which is to take a well-filled barley grain and cut it in two. A white colour means that it's suitable for milling and conversion. This simple test is as relevant today as it was many years ago.

▼ Mill for unmalted barley, wheat and rye, at Kilbeggan the oldest licensed whiskey distillery in Ireland.

Blended Irish whiskeys

Irish malts have not developed in the same way that Scotch malts have, so you will not find many on shelves around the world, but the industry has successfully developed the blended trade. And now the blends are what Ireland is most famous for. Their capacity for producing two different flavours within the same stillhouse (one flavour produced, for example, by combining the effects of a big fat still with two small thin stills, the other by combining a tall, bulbous still with a small thin one and a big fat one) has imbued them with a flexibility envied around the world.

Black Bush (Bushmills)
A blend from Bushmills distillery with a relatively high (70 per cent or more) malt content and aged for longer than average, predominantly in sherry cask. This has a sweet, rich and sherried nose with fresh, malty, fudge and toffee flavour with a little crisp gooseberry fruit; finishing with some chocolate.

Bushmills White Label (Midleton)
Also known as 'White Bush', this is a blend of malt whiskey from the distillery of the same name and grain whiskey from Midleton. It is malty with some oaky vanilla and honey and a floral touch; the flavour is clean, medium-dry and simple with some elderflower finishing with a spicy note.

Clontarf Classic (Clontarf Distilling Company)

Medium-bodied with a touch of smoke, orange and spirity toffee; the flavour is medium-bodied and medium-sweet with butterscotch, toffee and a light touch of smoke. It finishes sweet with a touch of spice.

Crested Ten (Pernod Ricard)

Big and impressive with hazelnutty sherry notes and ginger; the flavour is smooth with honey, toffee and chocolate; finishing dry and clean.

Green Spot (Pernod Ricard)

Medium-bodied and fresh with new-mown grass, mint, honey and cocoa notes; it is mouth-wateringly zingily fresh and clean, with rich heather honey and spice finishing long, elegant and hedgerow leafy with an espresso note.

Jameson's 12 Years Old (Pernod Ricard)

The sherry cask influence is instantly noticeable, nutty, raisined and sweet, then the whiskey takes over with crisp appley fruit dipped in honey and coated in vanilla.

Kilbeggan Blend (Cooley)

Clean and citrusy lime and some apple on the nose, with medium-sweet, smooth toasted malt and some honey on the palate, which finishes rich with a fresh greenness and some spicy oak.

Murphy's (Pernod Ricard)

Quite light with toffee/fudge and some varnish with a hint of peanut butter; the flavour is grassy and gooseberry-fruited finishing clean and lightly spicy with some soft vanilla.

Paddy's (Pernod Ricard)

Medium-bodied with floral and apple/peach overtones, its flavour is medium-dry and perfumed with soft, smooth oaky vanilla toffee notes finishing dry and malty.

Power's (Pernod Ricard)

Clean, fresh and with a little honeyed floral note and crisp, zesty citrus cereals; the flavour is medium-dry and of medium weight with some beeswax and leathery oak; finishing very crisp, fresh dry and clean.

Redbreast (Pernod Ricard)

Honeyed and fruity with intense grapefruit and gooseberry notes, some clean, sherried hazelnuts and rich, creamy fruitcake; the flavour is big-bodied, spicy, gingery, dark, sherried brazil nuts, all swimming in treacle and finishing long and complex with liquorice and Chinese spices.

Tullamore Dew (William Grant)

Grassy and gooseberried with some toasty oak notes; the flavour is medium-bodied, medium-sweet and fruity with caramel, cinnamon and some sherry rubber finishing long, sweet and beeswax-coated.

4

North America

Bourbon production

American whiskey reflects the production techniques of Scotland and Ireland because Scottish and Irish settlers brought their making skills with them to the USA. Thus, it was natural that America's indigenous grains should be distilled into American whiskeys.

You will find some similarities of flavour to Scotch and Irish whiskeys, but also that the very different climatic conditions in the Americas impose a different character on the spirit. The heat means that long maturation is very unusual in America. Obviously, the different mix of grains has a bearing on the final flavour also. American whiskeys are more robust than their Scottish and Irish counterparts and can assimilate the overpowering influence of new wood, without the whiskeys' flavours being swamped by the oak. If Scotch and Irish whiskeys are matured in new wood, the flavours are completely dominated by the oak's characters.

The father of Bourbon

The practice of charring barrels was established in 1789 when there was a fire in a barn used by Elijah Craig, a Baptist minister and farmer, to store empty whiskey barrels. Craig put his new make into the burnt barrels and discovered that his whiskey was ageing better than it had done in new oak casks. It picked up more colour and flavour, and his discovery earned Craig the title of 'The Father of Bourbon'.

Classifying a bourbon

Bourbon need not come from Bourbon County in Kentucky, and can be made in almost any part of the United States.

In 1791 Congress imposed an excise tax on whiskey, inciting the 'Whiskey Rebellion', a part of which was the Boston Tea Party, and led to the migration of north-eastern distillers into Kentucky. At one point, there were 2,000 US distilleries producing bourbon; following Prohibition, there are now no more than a dozen in Kentucky.

Generally a bourbon's first distillation takes place in a column still, and the second distillation occurs in a 'doubler' still, which is a pot still.

To be called a bourbon, the spirit must:

• be produced in the USA

• be produced from a mashbill consisting of at least 51 per cent corn

• be distilled to a strength of no more than 160 proof (80 per cent ABV)

• be matured in new, charred, white oak barrels at no more than 125 proof (62.5 per cent ABV)

• have nothing added to the final product except pure water

• state the duration of its ageing on its label, if aged for less than four years (if aged for a minimum of two years, it may be called 'straight bourbon')

• be bottled at a minimum alcoholic strength of 80 proof (40 per cent ABV).

▼ Flames shoot from the top of bourbon barrels as they are fired and charred at the Brown-Forman Cooperage in Louisville, Kentucky.

Kentucky bourbons

Barton distillery

BARDSTOWN, KENTUCKY

Originally founded by Tom Moore in 1879, the current utilitarian distillery was built in 1946. Its fermenters and stills are constructed from stainless steel, the sole concessions to tradition are the doubler still and the copper tops of the beer stills.

Kentucky Gentleman

The nose is a little dumb with some sweet oak and toffee, while the flavour is big and hits the palate suddenly opening out to sweet, ripe citrus and cherry fruit backed by some oak and maple syrup. It finishes well, but dry with an oily, oaky, nutty character.

Jim Beam distillery

CLERMONT, KENTUCKY, WWW.JIMBEAM.COM

Originally farmers in Kentucky's bluegrass hills, the Beams began distilling in 1795. They have been using successive strains of the same yeast for the past 75 years. As the world's best-selling bourbon, they filled their 10 millionth barrel in 2005.

Knob Creek

Rich and ripe, intensely sweet aromas of marmalade, buttery vanilla with a little almond and a hint of char; the flavour is delicate, but complex with chocolate and spice, apple and some gently chewy, nutty oak; finishing with marshmallows, cocoa and great length.

Buffalo Trace distillery

FRANKFORT, KENTUCKY,

WWW.BUFFALOTRACEDISTILLERY.COM

Buffalo Trace has had many names over the years, from Old Fire Copper, through Old Stagg, Ancient Age and finally, Buffalo Trace in 1999 in memory of the buffalo herds that used to cross the Kentucky River close by. All their whiskeys are of the small batch variety.

George T Stagg 15 Years Old

This is the 2009 release of the 15 years old. The nose is complex: mint, toffee, leather, cinnamon, chocolate, marmalade and maple syrup; the corn flavour has spice with tangerines, cocoa, coffee and finishes with quite an alcoholic burn, which seems well-balanced with sweet tobacco and toffee-dipped cherries.

Four Roses distillery

LAWRENCEBURG, KENTUCKY,

WWW.FOURROSESBOURBON.COM

The buildings at the distillery are unique in distilling as well as in Kentucky, being built in a Spanish Mission style. The company combines five proprietary yeast strains with two separate mashbills to produce 10 distinct and handcrafted bourbon recipes, each with its own unique character.

Four Roses Single Barrel

Rich and quite restrained, perfumed, floral, with spice, nutmeg, creamy vanilla toffee, orange and lime; the flavour is smooth, soft and rounded, medium-dry with some sweet mint and buttery, toasted vanilla; finishing gently chewy with a hit of cinnamon and the toast lingering.

Heaven Hill distillery

BARDSTOWN, KENTUCKY, WWW. HEAVENHILL.COM

In 1935, the Shapira brothers opened Heaven Hill distillery. They filled their 6 millionth barrel in November 2010. The distillery experienced a huge fire in 1996, which consumed a number of full warehouses and saw a paved road melt under the river of burning whiskey. Despite this, the company survived; the warehouses have been rebuilt, stocks have been replaced and sales continue to grow.

Elijah Craig 18 Years Old Single Barrel

Imposing, complex and intense: custard, bananas, coconut, buttery popcorn and creamy toffee apples;

the flavour is medium-sweet and smoky spicy with lemony citrus and gently chewy oaky crème brûlée vanilla; finishing extremely elegant and well-balanced with maple oak and a distinctly smoky tail.

Maker's Mark distillery

LORETTO, KENTUCKY, WWW.MAKERSMARK.COM

In 1953, Bill Samuels Sr bought the Buck's Spring distillery in Happy Hollow. He dropped the rye from his mashbill and substituted wheat: 70 per cent corn, 14 per cent wheat and 16 per cent malted barley, a formula that continues to this day.

Maker's Mark

Soft, sweet, ripe corn and bubble gum; with water, demerara sugar, honey, shellac varnish, red-skinned apples and ripe pineapple come out; the flavour is medium-bodied, medium-sweet and rich with a little spicy, oily vanilla and some caramelized red fruits. The finish is long, perfumed, elegant and soft with a touch of maple syrup and butterscotch.

Maker's 46

This is a Maker's Mark fully matured for a few months more, in contact with seared French oak staves. Rich, ripe and more refined than usual Maker's Mark; water brings out toffee apples, honey, home baking, creamy vanilla and liquorice; the flavour is drier than Maker's Mark and it grows in the mouth with gently chewy oak, good body, spice and honey; finishing long, very elegant and ethereal, flowing into tangy spice on the tail.

Climate control and cask creativity

Most Kentucky whiskeys are aged in rick warehouses up to nine storeys high, with barrels stacked three high on each floor.

Kentucky has hot summers and cold winters, causing the top floors to bake in the summer heat while the ground floor stays cool. In winter the top floor retains some heat while the ground is cold.

As a result, the whiskey on each floor matures at a different rate: the barrels on the top floor mature faster than those on the bottom.

The Kentuckians have dealt with the problem in several ways. By opening windows they allow air to circulate and dissipate the summer's heat. Some distillers move their barrels between the floors, levelling out the maturation, while others blend whiskeys from each floor to maintain consistency.

The premium blends and small batch bottling come from the middle floors where the temperature fluctuations are less extreme.

There is also a great deal of experimentation going on with barrels in the whiskey world at the moment, and it's not just a case of keeping the whiskey in the cask for a couple of years longer.

Maker's 46 is a prime example. Whiskey maker, Kevin Smith explains: 'We started off trying smaller barrels; we tried bigger barrels; we tried cubes; we tried all sorts of things.

When the cooperage offered us the Profile 46 stave (that had been seared on the outside), it caused the flavours that we were looking for: the oak toasted aromas to come through, those deeper, richer, vanilla/caramel notes.

And the most amazing piece was that the spiciness that came out of it wasn't bitter. The flavours coming through are reminiscent of Maker's Mark, but what we've done is add a little more spice, but no tannins. None of these changes make it necessarily better, it is just a slightly different Maker's Mark.'

▶ Oak barrels in the ageing warehouse, Woodford Reserve distillery, Versailles, Kentucky, USA.

Wild Turkey distillery

LAWRENCEBURG, KENTUCKY, WILDTURKEYBOURBON.COM

Founded in 1869, the distillery sits 80 m above the Kentucky River. It was not until 1940 that the brand was created after a distillery executive took some of the whiskey on an annual wild turkey shoot. His friends enjoyed it so much that, the following year, they asked him to bring that same 'Wild Turkey' bourbon along with him and the brand was born.

Wild Turkey 8 Years Old 101

Medium-bodied, delicate and subdued with creamy vanilla leather; with water, orange marmalade and baked apples with cinnamon on buttery toast comes out; the flavour is medium-dry, rich with dry tannins and tingling spice; finishing long, smooth and elegant with creamy oak, ending dry on the tail. Despite the high strength (50.5 per cent ABV), the alcohol is well integrated into the flavour.

▲ The bourbon tasting room at Woodford Reserve distillery, Versailles, Kentucky, USA.

Woodford Reserve distillery

VERSAILLES, KENTUCKY, WWW.WOODFORDRESERVE.COM

Originally called the Oscar Pepper distillery when erected in 1838, it was renamed Woodford Reserve distillery in 1996. Woodford uses three copper pot stills and its spirit is produced using triple distillation.

Woodford Reserve

Rich, orange, charred vanilla oak with dark chocolate dipped raisins, ginger and vanilla; the flavour is full of soft, subtle spices with toasted sweetcorn, raspberries and demerara finishing with creamy toffee, butterscotch, comb honey and a floral flourish.

Other Bourbons

A. Smith Bowman distillery
FREDERICKSBURG, VIRGINIA, WWW.ASMITHBOWMAN.COM

Built in 1935 in Fairfax County, the distillery was
moved 60 miles to the north to its present location,
in response to growth in 1988.

Bowman Brothers Virginia Bourbon
Sweetcorn surprisingly and an almost rhubarb
crumble fruitiness and freshness with a creamy butter
touch; the flavour is sweet, smooth and of medium to
good body with a little oaky vanilla; finishing with
some heat and fresh fruit.

Tuthilltown Spirits distillery
GARDINER, NEW YORK, WWW.TUTHILLTOWN.COM

Set up in 2003, Tuthilltown became New York's first
distillery since Prohibition, prior to which, according
to the company, there were 'upwards of 1,000 farm
stills'. They produce small amounts using harvests
from the farms in the area around the distillery.

Hudson's Four Grain Bourbon
(2010 bottling)
Juicy slices of orange sitting on top of creamy,
buttered toast with a drizzle of maple syrup, it has a
floral note and hint of fresh peach; the flavour is
smooth and of spicy sweetcorn and fresh citrus
finishing with mouth-watering, zesty orange and
toasted marshmallows.

Tennessee style

The difference between bourbon and Tennessee whiskeys is that Tennessee whiskey is filtered through 3 m of maple charcoal. The company claims that Jack Daniels discovered the process, but it is also claimed that the practice was already common even before 1825, when it was recorded that Alfred Eaton had adopted the process.

Jack Daniels distillery

LYNCHBURG, MOORE COUNTY, TENNESSEE,
WWW.JACKDANIELS.COM

The world's largest whiskey distiller, their annual production is now 180 million litres of alcohol and sales are in excess of 10 million cases per annum.

▼ The charcoal mellowing building, where every drop of Jack Daniels is dripped through 3 m of charcoal.

The population of Lynchburg is currently around a mere 500 of whom Jack Daniels employ 370. Moore County is a 'dry' county and the distillery visitor shop is the only outlet in Moore County that is permitted to sell liquor. It is also the top-selling liquor outlet in the state of Tennessee.

▲ Jack Daniels' signature is embossed on every single bottle neck.

Jack Daniels Single Barrel

For a distillery with an output as large as JD's, it is astounding that they can be bothered with such small volume bottling runs as Single Barrel. Cherries, American cream soda, coconut, some smoky cough linctus character; the flavour is sweet and spicy, of good body, rich and chocolate orange; finishing with some spicy caramel oak and a floral note on the tail.

George Dickel distillery

CASCADE HOLLOW, TULLAHOMA, TENNESSEE,
WWW.GEORGEDICKEL.COM

In 1870, George Dickel set up as a distiller at Cascade
Hollow on the Highland Rim of the Cumberland
Plateau. A great experimenter, he found that the
whisky (spelt this way as he felt that his whisky was
comparable to Scotch whisky) he made in the winter
was smoother than the summer's distillation, so he
chilled his whisky before it went into the charcoal
mellowing vats. The practice filters out the oils and
fatty acids inherent in most whiskey products.

George Dickel No. 12
Quite soft, sweet and buttery with walnut, peanut,
toffee and sweetcorn over charred oak; the flavour is
of good weight, sweet, muscovado sugar with dried
banana and coconut, vanilla oak and custard and
darker treacle, finishing with a note of cinnamon,
some raisins, caramel, honey and the char replaying.

George Dickel Barrel Select
Quite delicate, but charred oaky vanilla initially
opening to leather, orange and liquorice; the flavour
is soft, smooth and medium-bodied with sweet maple
syrup, peppery spices and beeswax; finishing quite
elegantly ethereal with toffeeyed oak char and some
citrus freshness.

Rye whiskey

Rye must be made from a mashbill containing a minimum of 51 per cent rye and must be matured in new oak barrels. It makes a great base for cocktails because rye gives a more spicy and characterful flavour.

Jim Beam Rye
Peppery rye and a little toffee apple and dried banana; the flavour is fresh, but light and smooth with a little orange finishing with medium length, some fennel and a little sweetness.

Pikesville Rye
Produced by Heaven Hill in the Maryland style. Quite full, with caramel, leathery oak and acetone

▼ Pikesville Rye Whiskey, 110 proof.

and ripe pears at the back; the flavour is medium-sweet and of good weight with peppery spice, beeswax and a dried apple note, and it finishes with the peppery rye and some citrus.

Rittenhouse Rye
Produced by Heaven Hill, in the style of the classic Pennsylvania or 'Monongahela' rye whiskeys. Big and sweet, orange marmalade and ginger, cocoa/chocolate and toasted leather; the flavour is also quite big-bodied with dried citrus fruits, demerara sugar, apples and molasses; finishing dryish and spicy with a pleasant bitterness.

Sazerac Rye
Distilled by Buffalo Trace. Sweet vanilla spices leap out of the glass, followed by cloves, pepper and cinnamon; the flavour is warm, medium-sweet and rich with citrus and dipping toffee, finishing lingeringly and quite complex with liquorice and a touch of paprika.

Van Winkle Family Reserve
This is a 13 Year Old whiskey produced at Buffalo Trace. Quite big with vanilla, sweetcorn, milk chocolate/cocoa, leather and peppery spice; the flavour is medium-sweet with cherries, toffee apple and a hazelnut note. It finishes well with a hint of alcohol and caramel oak notes.

Other whiskey styles

Micro-distillation of whiskey has developed on the back of micro-brewing and fruit spirit distillation in the USA, as elsewhere. The emphasis is on the 'micro', with bottling runs being tiny and the consequent lack of availability of the whiskey.

Anchor Distilling Co.
SAN FRANCISCO, CALIFORNIA,
WWW.ANCHORDISTILLING.COM

A micro-brewery at the heart of San Franciso, Anchor branched out into micro-distilling in 1993 with the installation of small copper pot stills.

Old Potrero Rye
Very smoky and similar to Scotch. Old leather and demerara sugar with some cinnamon; the flavour is rich and Christmas cake fruity, buttery and spicy; finishing sweet with spiced fruits and a hint of smoke on the tail.

Clear Creek distillery
PORTLAND, OREGON, WWW. CLEARCREEKDISTILLERY.COM

Originally developed by Steve McCarthy, to produce fruit spirits from his family's orchards. He picked up a taste for peated whiskey after a wet visit to Ireland. His wash is produced by a local brewery.

McCarthy's Oregon Single Malt

Medium-bodied and youthful with a slightly green vegetal note, some apple, an earthily smoky peat note, a hint of rubber and some candle wax; the flavour is medium-sweet and fresh with good peat integration, a touch of tarry rope and toffee and ripe citrus; finishing long, squeaky clean, rich and herby with bergamot and tea on the tail.

St George Spirits
ALAMEDA, CALIFORNIA, WWW.STGEORGESPIRITS.COM

Set up in 1982 by Jörg Rupf from Alsace to distil eaux de vie. Having produced fruit spirits (a great deal of experimentation goes on in Alameda), it was natural that they should branch out into whiskey.

St George Californian Single Malt

Very fruity – lime/cherries/red fruits – and a winey note with some buttery toffee and bubble gum; the flavour is medium-sweet with apples, blackberries, cloves, liquorice and finishes with a little Szechuan spice and a reprise of the cherry bubble gum.

To ice, or not to ice?

Some people frown on putting ice or water into whisky, but it's all a matter of personal taste, circumstance, and the type of whisky. Jeff Arnett, Master Distiller at Jack Daniels, has this to say:

'I drink Jack Daniels' Single Barrel, "on the rocks". This is a travesty according to some drinkers from the world's cooler countries as they claim that the addition of ice kills the flavour. I agree that too much ice can dull the whiskey's more subtle flavours, but that doesn't mean you can't add any.

Tennessee's climate is too hot to not add ice – the summer temperatures are regularly in excess of 26°C (80°F) and often remain at that level for several weeks on end – so I drink it on the rocks to cool me down. In the winter it gets cold so I drink it neat when I need warming up. At the end of the day, the final choice of how you drink it is up to you; your palate dictates your method of enjoyment.'

Canada

Settlers from the Old World brought their distilling experiences with them and Canada's vast acreage of grain production gave them cereals aplenty to mash. Canadian whiskies are blended. Each grain gives a different character, as does each barrel.

Alberta distillery

CALGARY, ALBERTA, WWW.ALBERTARYE.COM

Calgary is too cold to grow corn, so the whiskies produced here have always had a high rye content. Rye whiskies are not to everyone's taste, corn has a soft, lighter, easier-drinking style of whisky, but Alberta has doggedly stuck with their spicy style.

Alberta Premium

A little subdued with a floral touch, some honeyed toffee, chocolate and glucose confectionery; the flavour is mellow, medium-sweet with some ginger and has a smooth and spicy rye bite and creamy vanilla, finishing cleanly and of medium length.

Canadian Mist distillery

COLLNGWOOD, ONTARIO, WWW.CANADIANMIST.COM

The stills here are outwardly made of shiny stainless steel, but their innards are constructed out of copper, so that the spirt is in contact with copper all through the distillation process. The spirit is triple-distilled and their mashbill is corn and barley to which a little rye whisky made onsite is added.

Canadian Mist

Medium-bodied with a grassy fruitiness, lemons, oranges, vanilla, a malty note and some cinnamon; the flavour is gentle, medium-sweet and soft with creamy vanilla toffee and zingily fresh orange and a little spice; finishing clean and peppery with a little reprise from the lemon.

Crown Royal distillery

GIMLI, ALBERTA, WWW.CROWNROYAL.COM

Known as Gimli distillery until recently, the current distillery was only opened in 1968, the whisky having been previously produced in the now-defunct Waterloo distillery in Ontario.

Crown Royal Cask No. 16

Medium-bodied, rich and with some spice – nutmeg, ginger and hazelnuts, green apples and a little peach; the flavour is sweet with juicy and zesty orange notes and softly chewy, creamy oak; finishing with buttery vanilla and a reprise of the sweet citrus.

Glenora distillery

GLENVILLE, INVERNESS COUNTY, NOVA SCOTIA,

WWW.GLENORADISTILLERY.COM

The distillery's make is a single malt produced in pot stills and is the only Scottish style single malt made in Canada. The distillery, which opened in 1990 and is attached to a country inn, has the capacity to produce 250,000 litres of alcohol a year but normally produces just 50,000 litres annually.

Glen Breton 10 Years Old Single Malt

Big-bodied, creamy vanilla and cereal notes, some butterscotch, honey and pine notes; the flavour is rich, medium-sweet and creamy with toffee and some chocolate spread on toast; finishing elegant, rounded and distinguished with a touch of sweetness and a breath of peat.

◄ The Glenora Distillery and Inn, Cape Breton Island, Nova Scotia, Canada.

Highwood distillery

HIGH RIVER, CALGARY,

WWW.HIGHWOOD-DISTILLERS.COM

A Canadian independent distiller, described as 'quirky'. Established in 1974 it was originally called 'Sunnyvale', but in 1984 was renamed 'Highwood Distillers' after the famous river. Highwood uses Canadian prairie wheat instead of corn in the mashbills for its whiskies.

Centennial 10 Years Old Rye

The nose is of apples and almonds sitting in toffee with a little garnish of orange peel; the flavour is fresh, smooth and medium-dry with beeswax and some black pepper; finishing cleanly with the spice tingling across your tongue.

Kittling Ridge distillery

GRIMSBY, ONTARIO

Whisky maker John Hall is an award-winning winemaker who has broadened his vision to produce a whisky from his pot still distillery at Lake Ontario. He distils and matures each grain separately and then blends them to produce his ultimate whisky.

Forty Creek Barrel Select

Rich and delicately sherried with a charred cask note and fruity – orange, cherry and chocolate with muscovado sugar; the flavour is rich and honeyed with butterscotch and coffee, finishing subtly and cleanly with a little cocoa on the tail.

Valleyfield distillery

SALABERRY-DE-VALLEYFIELD, QUEBEC

The V.O. stands for 'Very Own' and the brand was originally created for the Seagram family's exclusive use. The distillery is now owned by Pernod Ricard.

Seagram V.O.

Spicy, young, fruity, apples and apricot, integrated corn and cinnamon; the flavour is medium-dry and smooth with oranges, zingy acidity and honey; finishes clean and warm with a bitter touch to end.

▲ The bottling room at the Walkerville distillery, Ontario, 1911.

Walkerville distillery

WINDSOR, ONTARIO

Hiram Walker started construction near Windsor, Ontario in 1857. A town called Walkerville grew up around the distillery. During Prohibition in the USA, Canadian whisky became very popular and the proximity of Detroit made it easy for the company to profit from it.

Canadian Club

Sweetcorn/vanilla custard with some orange and spice; the flavour is medium-bodied, sweet and rye spicy supported by the malted barley and it finishes clean with some bitter rye.

Sampling a cask

In order to get a small amount out of a cask to sample, the industry developed a form of large pipette (known as a 'valinch' from the Gaelic in Scotland and Ireland and as a 'whiskey thief' in North America).

These are made of copper with a small hole at the bottom and a vent hole at the top. The implement is inserted in the cask and fills with whisky.

The sampler covers the top hole with his thumb, which creates a vacuum, holding the whisky within the tube, which can then be lifted out of the cask.

OBAN
1996

1996

OBAN DISTILLERY

5 Global Expansion

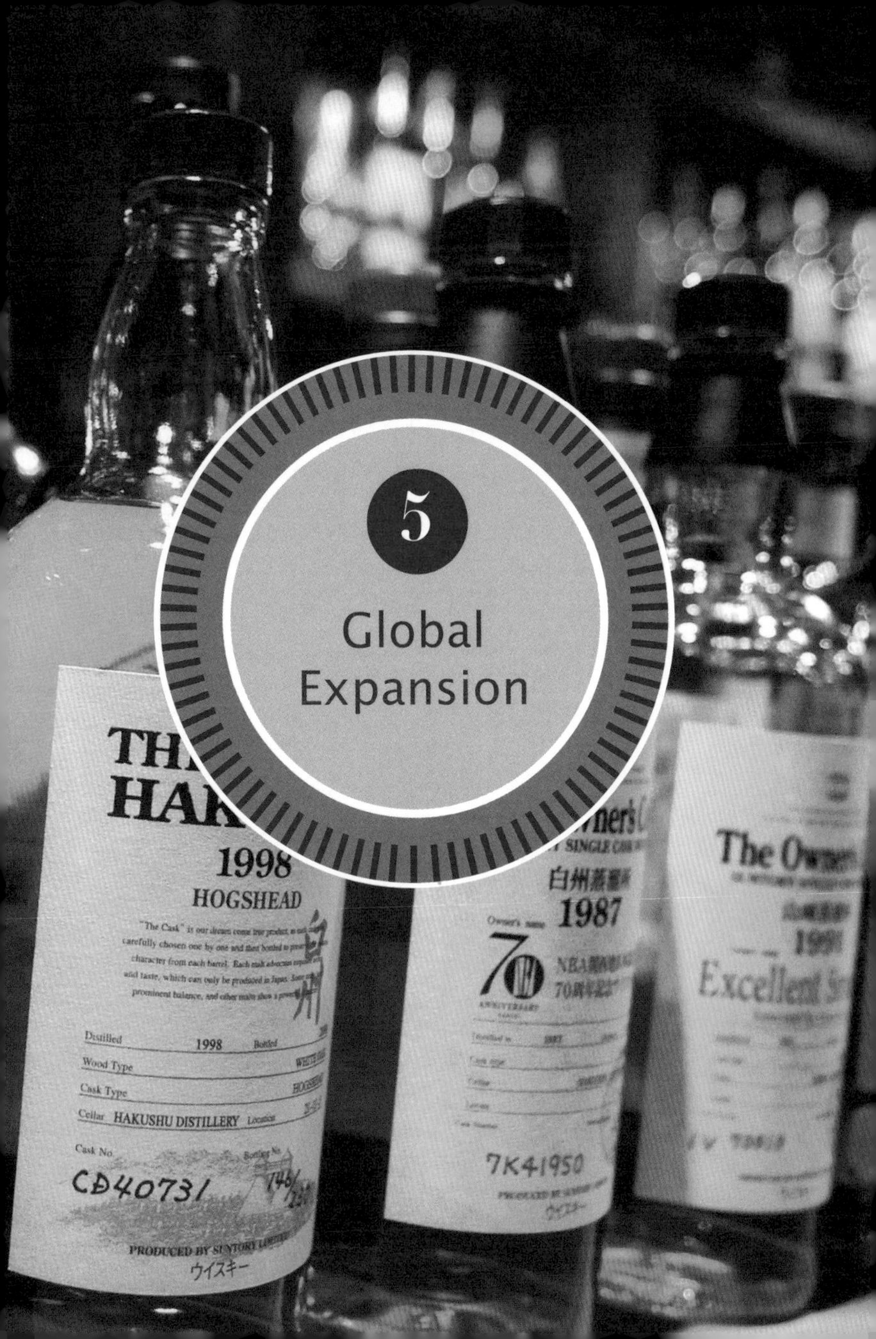

Europe

Although a little dwarfed by their close proximity to Scotland and Ireland, there are a growing number of whisky producers in Europe. Their spirits are largely produced for the local market but a good selection distribute globally.

Glann ar Mor distillery

CREC'H AR FUR, BRITTANY, WWW.GLANNARMOR.COM

Installed, in 2005, into a farmhouse that was built in 1668 in the Presqu'ile Sauvage (the Wild Peninsula) of northern Brittany. On a sea-battered coastline, a former advertising executive from Paris has established this distillery.

Glann ar Mor Second Bottling

Medium-bodied and fruity with a youthful bubble-gum note, cocoa comes out followed by desiccated coconut and acetone; the flavour is medium-sweet, of good weight and rich with a delicate peat note, some honey, bubblegum and slightly biscuity – chocolate digestives; finishing long, very clean and quite ethereal with a slight hint of menthol.

The Scotch Single Malt Circle

C/O W. MILLER, AUF DER HOFREITH 35, D- 40489, DÜSSELDORF, GERMANY, WWW.SCOTCHSINGLE.DE

Set up by Bill Miller and his wife Maggie in 1983 as a small club celebrating the produce of his homeland, the Circle now bottle a wide range of casks annually.

Zuidam distillery

BAARLE NASSAU, THE NETHERLANDS, WWW.ZUIDAM.EU

Established in 1975, the barley is ground using traditional Dutch windmills. The family began as distillers of genever and produced their first whisky in 2000. They have four small pot stills, which are also used for the production of their other spirits.

Millstone 8 Years Old French Oak

Medium-bodied and rich with good apple/peach and citrus fruit notes. There is a perfumed character, some floral notes and coconut sitting at the back; the flavour is dry, with good body, cocoa, cereal and dry paper; finishing long and dry with nutty toffee and coconut.

Mackmyra distillery

VALBO, SWEDEN, WWW.MACKMYRA.COM

Now 10 years old, Mackmyra was set up in a former power station. Juniper twigs are added to the peat when drying the malt and Swedish barley and Swedish oak casks are used. Maturation occurs in cool conditions 50 metres underground in a former mine.

Mackmyra Preludium 06

Forward fruit characters of lemon and pear backed by some juniper, toffee, honey and woodsmoke; the flavour is fresh, smoky and malty with a strong vanilla oak note and finishing with toasted oak and firm cinnamon spice.

Japan

The Japanese whisky industry began in 1929 and other countries have been quick to follow. In more recent years, the growth in boutique micro-distilleries has been quite amazing to see.

The industry developed out of the shochu and sake industries. Japanese distillers operate in a similar manner to the Irish in that they have a variety of different still shapes and styles in their stillhouses and by running the changes, can produce a wide variety of different flavours from the same stillhouse.

Chichibu distillery
CHICHIBU-SHI, SAITAMA

Japan's newest distillery, producing first in 2008, the washbacks are made of the local Mizunara oak and the stills are from Forsyths in Rothes, Aberlour.

Chichibu Newborn Cask no. 446

Quite big-bodied, sweet and rich with clean vanilla notes; with water, the bourbon notes really come out with hazelnut and maple predominating and a dark nutty note. The flavour is medium-dry, ripe, dark and smooth with honey and spice bouncing across the tongue and some rich butterscotch; finishing long and slightly perfumed, very softly chewy and quite ethereal.

Chichibu Heavily Peated

Quite big-bodied with a breakfast cereal note
and an aroma of smoked cheese, which becomes
more smoked ham with the addition of water; the
flavour is dry, quite rich and gently chewy with a
smoky cereal touch finishing long, powerful and
heavily smoked.

Hakushu Higashi distillery

HOKUTO, YAMANASHI-KEN

Built in 1981 to the west of the original Hakushu,
which now only produces whisky for blending.
Suntory have established a bird reserve around the
distillery, which is located in a forest at the southern
end of the Japanese Alps.

Hakushu 12 Years Old

Medium-bodied and quite delicate with notes of
peaches, orange blossom, honey and citrus zest. The
flavour is medium-dry and softly chewy showing
chocolate, a floral note and delicate peat; finishing
very well with quite smoky, cocoa-flavoured peat and
espresso coffee on the tail.

Yamazaki distillery

SHIMAMOTO-CHO, MISHAMA-GUN, OSAKA

Japan's first whisky distillery, set up by Shinjiro Torii
and Masataka Taketsuru in 1923 in an area that
is surrounded by three rivers, giving ideal
humidity. Owners Suntory use a lot of Mizunara
casks, the indigenous Japanese oak, for maturing
their whiskies.

Yamazaki 18 Years Old

Quite delicate with mature sherry notes, dried fruit, orange peel, honey and dark, but delicate peat; the flavour is medium-bodied, rich and medium-dry with a bit of spice, some citrus, dried fruit and a gentle brush of peat; finishing softly chewy, elegant and quite ethereal.

Yamazaki 1984

Lots of Mizunara flavour – sandalwood, incense, chocolate, liquorice opens out and there is creamy toffee, some orange and leathery vanilla; the flavour is medium-dry with Mizunara characters of pine, Japanese spices and nuts backed up by plum jam and treacle. It finishes long, big-bodied and complex.

Yoichi distillery

YOICHIGUN, YOICHIMACHI, KUROKAWACHO

WWW.NIKKA.COM/ENG

Founded in 1934 by Masataka Taketsuru near the neck of the Shakotan Peninsula. He started with one pot still, he did not have enough money for a second still until some years later. Both distillations were carried out in this one still. Taketsuru felt that the humidity, water supply and climate are similar to Scotland and the buildings have a very Scottish appearance.

Taketsuru 21 Years Old

Medium-bodied, rich, sweet, oily oak, peaches and
apricot jam, honey and beeswax opens out along
with buttery brioche / créme brûlée; the flavour is
smooth, medium-sweet and rounded with notes of
orange marmalade, ginger, bergamot and some spice;
finishing long, with sweet spices and apricot jam,
some fresh spearmint and a hit of peat.

▲ Barrels
stacked at
Yamazaki whisky
distillery, Japan.

The Rest of the World

Bakery Hill distillery

BALWYN NORTH, VICTORIA, AUSTRALIA,

WWW.BAKERYHILLDISTILLERY.COM.AU

Established in a north-eastern suburb of Melbourne
in 1999, their preferred strain of barley is the local
Schooner and Bakery Hill's whiskies mature quickly
because of the small size of their 50L or 100L casks.

Bakery Hill Cask Strength Peated Malt

Quite soft, delicate and medium-bodied with notes of
baked red-skinned apples with cloves and a delicate,
perfumed peat character; the flavour is medium-dry
with gently chewy apple skins, very Calvados-like
with some citrus and it finishes with a little touch of
spice, smoke and a touch of cocoa.

Tasmania distillery

CAMBRIDGE, TASMANIA,

WWW.SULLIVANSCOVEWHISKY.COM

Originally situated at Sullivan's Cove, the business
was purchased by a group of enthusiasts in 2003
and moved to Cambridge on the outskirts of Hobart.
Their wash is produced for them from the Franklin
strain of barley at Hobart's Cascade Brewery.

Sullivan's Cove Double Cask

Full and youthful with a chocolate malty note and
a rancio character; there are chocolate raisins, a
touch of citrus and rich, honeyed vanilla; the flavour

is medium-dry, rich and smooth with a smoky chocolate character; finishing with quite good length with a little touch of spice, some American cream soda and ripe peaches.

James Sedgwick distillery

WELLINGTON, SOUTH AFRICA,

WWW.THREESHIPSWHISKY.CO.ZA

This is the first blend of South African malt and grain whiskies. After initial maturation, the blend is filled into first fill bourbon casks for a further maturation.

Three Ships Bourbon Cask Finish

Vanilla oak, some perfume and spice, a very bourbon-influenced nose; the flavour is bourbon-like, with pepper, creamy vanilla and a floral touch to the finish, which is quite light and medium-dry with a touch of maple syrup.

Amrut distillery

RAJAJINIGAR, BANGALORE,

WWW.AMRUTDISTILLERIES.COM

Amrut first distilled whisky for blending in the early 1980s using barley grown in the Punjab and Rajasthan. Their first single malt was released in 2004.

Amrut Fusion

This is quite rich and toffeeyed with an orange perfume and a peat note, which floats above the rest; the flavour has fresh, leathery, beeswax-coated oak, is medium-dry, smooth and gently chewy and supported by creamy beeswax. It has a clean and very impressive finish with a tang of the peat smoke.

6

Discover

Enjoying whisky

Distillery employees spend many years of their life in a distillery. Over these years, their understanding and mastery of the process is enhanced and improved. All of this expertise goes into making the finest whisky possible for your drinking pleasure.

▶ A whisky tasting at the Whisky Shop Dufftown, Keith, Scotland.

However, some people focus on collecting whisky for its own sake, building up formidable collections of bottles of whiskies. Mainly because of this mania for collecting, the price of rare – and not so rare – bottlings has increased and, in some cases, increased quite considerably.

The product of certain distilleries, the Macallan and Bowmore to name but two, has leapt up in price in the past 20 years. Ardbeg has always been desirable for Islay fans; historically, this is because bottlings of the distillery's make were rare and new bottlings disappeared almost immediately.

Whisky, however, is meant to be drunk and enjoyed. It is a gregarious spirit meant for sharing in good company. It is not meant to sit in a bottle and be looked at – that would be a waste of the spirit-making expertise of all those distillery employees.

Bottlings and age

A company's core bottling is the one upon which their reputation depends. You will find therefore that this is its most consistent product, as it cannot afford to alienate those consumers who have come to rely on this brand as their 'usual'. Other bottlings will very often use a smaller, often considerably smaller, number of casks in their vatting. As such, there will be variations in colour and flavour between bottlings, but, as the market for these bottlings is (naturally) smaller and more informed, these variations are accepted and often even expected.

The more mature bottlings at, say 21, 25, 30 years old or older will differ from their predecesors. As a result of sales of that distillery's whiskies over the years and the amount that the angels consume, there is frequently a lack of availability of sufficient stocks of a particular colour or flavour profile and, in a 25 year old bottling, it may be necessary to include a cask of a 40 year old whisky, just to maintain some consistency in the bottling.

Life is easier for a blender putting together a vatting of, for example, Chivas Royal 25 Years Old. The blender will be able to change his recipe if whisky from distillery X is not available; by adding some from distillery Y and some from distillery Z, he can obtain the character he is looking for.

Buying at auction

Since the first dedicated whisky auction was held at Christie's in Bath Street, Glasgow in 1989, prices have escalated. Collectors from around the world have flocked to the auction houses to snap up the bargains to be had there. Nowadays, bidders for these magnificent bottlings no longer have to make the trek to Glasgow or Edinburgh to attend the auctions in person; they can stay at home and bid online. One benefit is that this means that the auction rooms should be less crowded, but it also means that there are more people bidding and likely to push up the prices of the bottles in which you are interested. This all means that, at the moment, the market in 'collectable' whiskies is very healthy, but as with any tradeable item, the value can go down as well as up.

▼ Sotheby's Hong Kong set a new record in 2014 when the Macallan M decanter by Lalique sold for £393,109.

Major auction houses

Bonham's – www.bonhams.com
Christie's – www.christies.com
McTear's – www.mctears.co.uk
Sotheby's – www.sothebys.com

Specialist retailers

Many retailers around the world offer a wide selection of whiskies from all corners of the world and, likewise, most will despatch to all corners of the world. The major retailers often have good websites.

SCOTLAND

Cadenhead's Whisky Shop
172 Canongate, Edinburgh, EH8 8BN

Canape Wines
85 Main Street, Bothwell, Glasgow,
G71 8ER
www.canapewines.co.uk

Duncan Taylor & Co. Ltd
4 Upperkirkgate, Huntly,
Aberdeenshire, AB54 8JU
www.duncantaylor.com

Eaglesome Ltd
30-32 Reform Square, Campbeltown,
Argyll, PA28 6JA

Gordon & MacPhail Ltd
58 South Street, Elgin, Moray,
IV30 1JY
www.gordonandmacphail.com

Loch Fyne Whiskies
Main St E, Inveraray, Argyll, PA32 8UD
www.lochfynewhiskies.co.uk

Luvian's Bottle Shop
93 Bonnygate, Cupar, Fife, KY15 4LG
www.luvians.com

Robbie's Dram
3 Sandgate, Ayr, KA7 1BG
www.robbieswhiskymerchants.com

Royal Mile Whiskies
379/381 High Street, Edinburgh,
EH1 1PW
www.royalmilewhiskies.com

Villeneuve Wines Ltd
1 Venlaw Court, Peebles, EH45 8AE
www.villeneuvewines.com

ENGLAND & WALES

Berry Bros. & Rudd
3 St James's Street, London,
SW1A 1EG
www.bbr.com

▶ Specialist retailers often stock miniatures of many brands, which is an excellent way to sample the vast array of whiskies available.

D Byrne & Co
12 King Street, Clitheroe, Lancashire,
BB7 2EP
www.dbyrne-finewines.co.uk

Cadenhead's Whisky Shop and
Tasting Room
26 Chiltern Street, London
W1U 7QF
www.whiskytastingroom.com

Dartmouth Vintners
The Butterwalk, 6 Duke Street,
Dartmouth, TQ6 9EB

Milroys
3 Greek St, Soho, London,
W1A 1ER
www.milroys.co.uk

The Vintage House
42 Old Compton St, Soho, London,
W1D 4LR
www.vintagehouse.co.uk

The Whisky Exchange
2 Bedford Street, Covent Garden,
London WC2E 9HH
www.thewhiskyexchange.com

The Wright Wine Co.
The Old Smithy, Raikes Rd, Skipton,
North Yorkshire,
BD23 1NP
www.wineandwhisky.co.uk

BELGIUM

Drankenshop Broekmans
Molenstraat 19, Zolder
www.drankenshop.be

CZECH REPUBLIC

Kratochvílovci
Chlumecká 765/6, 198 19 Praha 9
www.kratochvilovci.cz

DENMARK

Juul's Vinhandel
Værnedamsvej 15, 1819
Frederiksberg, Copenhagen
www.juuls.dk

FRANCE

La Maison du Whisky
20 rue d'Anjou, Paris
www.whisky.fr

GERMANY

Getränke Weiser
Darmstädter Str. 97, 64646
Heppenheim
www.thewhiskytrader.de

Weinquelle Lühmann
Lübecker Str. 145, 22067 Hamburg
www.weinquelle.com

Whisk(e)y Shop tara
Rindermarkt 16, 80331 München
www.whiskyversand.de

JAPAN

Liquors Hasegawa
Yaesu Shopping Mall, 2-1, Yaesu,
Chuo-ku, Tokyo
www.liquors-hasegawa.com

Liquor Villa Aizawa
570-9, Dairakuji-machi, Hachioji
www.aizawa-web.com

THE NETHERLANDS

Gall & Gall van der Boog
Dr H. Colijnlaan 289, Rijswijk
www.gall.nl

USA

Binny's Beverage Depot
300 North Clarke St, Lakeview,
IL 60657
www.binnys.com

D&M Wines & Liquors
2200 Fillmore Street, San Francisco,
CA 94115
www.dandm.com

Dundee Dell
5007 Underwood Ave, Omaha,
NE 68132
www.dundeedell.com

Park Avenue Liquor Shop
270 Madison Avenue, New York, NY
10016
www.parkaveliquor.com

The Whisky Shop
360 Sutter St, San Francisco,
CA 94108
www.whiskyshopusa.com

▲ Blending samples at Suntory Yamazaki malt whisky distillery, Japan.

Vintage and rare whiskies

As we have seen, any single cask bottling is, by its very nature, rare. The thickness of the staves, the number of cells in the wood, the location of the cask in the warehouse, the environment during maturation, the amount of handling the cask has received, climatic changes across the maturation period, even the length of time the whisky spends in a vat before being put into the bottle – all of these combine to create a totally unique flavour profile. The subtle nuances contained in the flavour of the whisky from that cask are not replicated in any of the casks filled on the same day and stored around it.

▲ Diageo
Managers'
Choice Series 27.

Single cask market

Many single cask bottlings are quite reasonably priced, especially from independent bottlers. Diageo's Managers' Choice bottling, on the other hand, is a total of 27 bottlings, one from each of Diageo's distilleries (apart from Roseisle, which only came on stream in 2009) and their price point is taking full advantage of the collectors' market.

An 8 Year Old Oban for £300 a bottle, for example, is excessive. The company argue that these are the finest examples of whisky from their respective distilleries, that collectors at auction would push the price up in any case and there are a very limited number of bottles available for the whole world. In the case of the Oban, there are 534 bottles, while the cask of Teaninch yielded a mere 246 bottles. From the company's declaration, it seems unlikely that many of these bottles will be drunk and that, in the fullness of time, most will pass beneath an auctioneer's gavel.

Vintage casks

As to vintage, the difference between the character of, say Scotland's excessively wet summer of 2010 and its excessively dry summer of 2003 has very little difference on the flavour except that the barley harvest in both vintages is put under stress. 2003 is reduced in size because of a lack of water and 2010 is reduced because of too much water in July and early August. Harvesting of summer barley in 2010, however was under good conditions, so the quality was good.

The Glenrothes distillery focuses on the vintage by only bottling their whisky when they think the casks are at their peak and identifying only the vintage year on most of their labels. It is difficult to make an argument for vintage variations because due to the difference in age, the cask influence varies from bottling to bottling. You will find nuances of difference between, for example, the 1994 and the 1991, but a great many of these differences are down to the influence of the wood.

Similarly, Balblair is only available by the vintage and, for the three vintages of Balblair currently available, 1975, 1989 and 2000, Andy MacDonald, the distillery manager, nosed 1062 casks to select a mere 81 casks for bottling.

▲ The 1989 casks in the Balblair distillery barrel-ageing store.

Storing whisky

There is not the same storage difficulty with whisky that there is with wine.

Oxidization is not so much of a problem, but, as with all alcohols, oxygen is a killer – alcohol and oxygen react to form acetic acid and water. Which means that, as soon as the bottle is opened, deterioration begins, as acetic acid and water is vinegar. With a bottle of wine, this may take 48 hours, the higher alcohol content of whisky means that you may have as long as two years before it deteriorates to any great extent.

This also means that many bars, where a large number of spirits are offered, are offering a product that is past its best. Superior outlets, such as The Highlander Inn in Craigellachie on Speyside, impose a sell by date on their bottles and they cut the price of whiskies as they near that sell by date in order to turn the stock over. In the case of The Highlander, they put a label on each bottle showing the date it was opened and, if it is not totally consumed within one year, it is consigned to kitchen duty.

Storage time

If unopened, a bottle can be stored almost indefinitely. Obviously, it should not be stored for a long period in direct sunlight. The liquid does not like that and the label will fade, reducing the

value. If you are storing a bottle to benefit from its appreciation in value, it is essential that the carton, if any, is also stored and kept in good condition. The easiest way to do this is to store it in a cool, darkened area and wrap each item in cling film. This protects labels, cartons and seals from unwelcome intrusion by beast, insects and humans.

▲ Not everyone can have a vaulted room especially for whisky such as this in Corgarff Castle, Aberdeenshire, but always store yours in a cool, darkened area.

Whisky cocktails

Whiskies have long been a base for classic cocktails from sours and Manhattans to more exotic concoctions. These recipes make one cocktail.

Cold Kiss

2 teaspoons of white Crème de Menthe
4½ cl Jameson's
1½ cl Peppermint Schnapps

Shake with crushed ice and strain into a tall glass. Garnish with mint.

Golden Glory

3 cl bourbon
3 cl Amontillado Sherry
3 cl dry vermouth

Stir in a mixing glass with ice and strain into a cocktail glass. Squeeze zest of orange over the top.

Rob Roy

3 cl Scotch whisky
3 cl sweet vermouth
A dash of Angostura Bitters

Stir in a glass with ice and strain into cocktail glass.

Don Pedro

3 cl Kahlua
240 g vanilla ice cream
3 cl Chivas Regal
1 tablespoon cream

Mix the ingredients in a blender and serve in a tall glass.

Whisky Sour

4½ cl whisky
4½ cl lemon juice
2¼ cl sugar syrup

Shake ingredients in a shaker with ice cubes. Strain into a tall glass. Garnish with a maraschino cherry.

Mountain Dew

6 cl Manzana Apple liqueur
3 cl Maker's Mark
3 cl whipped cream
Lemonade (7-up)

Shake with crushed ice, strain and pour over ice in a tall glass. Garnish with a twist of lime.

Red Scotch

3 cl Cutty Sark
3 cl tomato juice
Juice of half a lemon
A dash of Worcester-shire sauce
A dash of Tabasco

Shake the ingredients. Pour over ice into a tall glass. Decorate with freshly ground black pepper.

Mint Julep

3 cl of a peated Scotch Whisky
A dash of rhubarb bitters,
A cube of sugar
Mint
St Germain elderflower liqueur

Shake with crushed ice and serve in a tall glass with a garnish of mint. Serve with a straw.

Manhattan

6 cl rye whiskey
3 cl dry vermouth
A dash of Angostura Bitters

Shake with ice and strain into a cocktail glass. Garnish with a slice of lemon peel.

Shamrock

3 cl Irish whiskey
3 cl dry vermouth
3 dashes green chartreuse
3 dashes green Crème de Menthe

Stir in a glass with ice and strain into cocktail glass.

International appreciation

The only way to fully appreciate a whisky is to visit its home, the spot on this earth where the spirit has been created. Regrettably, most distilleries experience a dimunition of water supply in the warmer summer months and this is the time when whisky aficionados tend to make a pilgrimage to their distillery of choice. Because of this low water supply, distilleries have a 'silent season': a number of weeks during this warmer period when they shut down production to carry out essential maintenance; to permit the staff to take their holidays; and to allow their water supply to return to a higher level. Thus, many whisky tourists are disappointed when they arrive at the distillery to discover it quiet. Fortunately, many distilleries appreciate this and have interesting visitor centres to make the whisky tourist feel that his journey has not been wasted.

Tasting events

There are many tasting events around the world, such as Whisky Live! in Tokyo in February, the Annual Whiskies of the World Expo in San Francisco in March, WhiskyFest in Chicago in April, the Limburg Whisky Fair in Germany in May, Stockholm Whisky and Beer Festival in Sweden in September or Leiden International Whisky Festival in the Netherlands in November. The Scotch Malt Whisky Society holds regular tastings at both its locations around the world and in other suitable venues, so

you may find that there is one being held near to you. They are well worth attending as the Society's staff are knowledgeable and experienced at delivering a memorable evening. The world's various distilling companies also run events and tickets tend to be sold through whisky specialists in the local area.

▲ Whisky tasting room at Glengoyne Distillery, Scotland.

Whisky Live International Tasting Events
www.whiskylive.com

WhiskyFest USA
www.maltadvocate.com
www.whiskyfestblog.com

Scotch Malt Whisky Society
www.smws.co.uk

Speyside Whisky Festival
www.spiritofspeyside.com

World's best whisky bars

Whisky is a gregarious spirit and craves company. Where better to experience that company than in the ambience of one of the world's finest whisky bars?

UK

ALBANNACH
66 Trafalgar Square, London
WC2N 5DS

THE ANDERSON
Union Street, Fortrose, Ross-shire,
IV10 8TD

BON ACCORD
153 North Street, Glasgow, G3 7DA

DRUMCHORK LODGE HOTEL
Aultbea, Wester Ross, IV22 2HU

THE FISHERMAN'S RETREAT
Riding Head Lane, Shuttleworth,
Lancs., BL0 0HH

THE GRILL
213 Union Street, Aberdeen,
AB11 6BA

THE HIGHLANDER INN
Craigellachie, Banffshire, AB38 9SR

LOCHSIDE HOTEL
Shore Street, Bowmore, Isle of Islay,
PA43 7LB

THE MASH TUN
8 Broomfield Square, Aberlour,
Banffshire, AB38 9QP

ST ANDREWS BAR
37 Sunnyside Street, Coatbridge,
ML5 3DG

TAYCHREGGAN HOTEL
4 Ellieslea Road, Broughty Ferry,
Dundee, DD5 1JG

WHISKI
119 High Street, The Royal Mile,
Edinburgh, EH1 1SG

THE COLEY BAR
Caledonian Hotel, Princes Street,
Edinburgh, EH1 2AB

BELGIUM

BRUGS WHISKYHUIS
Cordoeaniersstraat 4, 8000 Brugge

CANADA

THE DAM PUB
53 Bruce Street, Thornbury, Ontario

FRANCE

WALLACE BAR
2 Rue Octavio Mey, Lyon 69005

GERMANY

GEIST IM GLAS
8.7 Lenaustr. 27 (Kottbusser Damm),
Berlin

SCOTCH & SOFA
8.2 Kollwitzstr. 18, Berlin

BERLVIN WHISKY & WEIN
7.6 Knaackstr. 70, Berlin

ITALY

BARMETRO
Via dei Martinitt, 3, Milan

IRELAND

BUSHMILLS INN
9 Dunluce Road, Bushmills, Northern
Ireland, BT57 8QG

THE BEAUFORT BAR
Beaufort, Killarney, Co. Kerry

**O'LOCLAINN'S IRISH
WHISKEY BAR**
Ballyvaughan, Co. Clare

THE TEMPLE BAR
47/48 Temple Bar, Dublin

JAPAN

BAR TALISKER
Fujihira Building, B1F 7-5-12 Ginza,
Chuo-Ku, Tokyo

THE HARBOUR INN
Shibata 1-3-7 Shibata, Kita-ku, Osaka

THE HIGHLANDER INN
Musashi-ya, 2-1-6 Chuo, Nakano-ku,
Tokyo

THE MASH TUN
Kami-Osaki 2F, Shinagawa-ku, Tokyo

THE NETHERLANDS

HOTEL FIDDER KON
Wilhelminastraat 6, 8019 AM Zwolle

NORTH END PUB
Noordeinde 55, 2311 CB, Leiden

WHISKYCAFE L&B
Korte Leidsedwarsstr 82–84, 1017 RD
Amsterdam

SOUTH AFRICA

BASCULE
Cape Grace, West Quay Road, Cape
Town

WILD ABOUT WHISKY
Auldstone House, 506, Naledi Drive,
Dullstroom

USA

CURRAGH IRISH PUB
73 East 8th Street, Holland, MI 49423

**ST. ANDREWS RESTAURANT
& BAR**
140 West 46th Street, New York, NY,
10036

Whisky societies

A great way to enjoy whiskies is through the various whisky societies around the world. Many of these are run by retailers, such as Drambusters in Dumfries, Scotland.

Other than these, there are many societies who meet in most whisky-drinking countries around the world. Some of these are listed below. Their websites will tell you when and where their next meetings are taking place.

AUSTRALIA
Malt Whisky Society of Australia
www.mwsoa.org.au

BELGIUM
The Wee Dram Whisky Society
www.weedram.be

CANADA
Companions of the Quaich
www.thequaich.com

CHINA
Shanghai Malt Club
www.maltclub.com

GERMANY
The Single Malt Whisky Club
www.single-malt-whisky-club.de

ITALY
Glu Glu 2000
www.gluglu2000.it

THE NETHERLANDS
International Whisky Society
www.internationalwhiskysociety.nl

SWITZERLAND
Swiss Whisky Society
www.whiskysociety.ch

USA
The Whisky Guild
www.whiskyguild.com/
whiskynetwork/home

Los Angeles Whiskey Society
www.lawhiskeysociety.com

Useful contacts

Most of the world's whiskies and distilleries have websites and some of them are very good, informative and imaginative, while others are simply basic vehicles for the brand. They are normally good at updating information about current bottlings and often include up to the minute information and news of events at the distillery or bottling plant. Other sources of information are:

The Scotch Whisky Association
www.scotch-whisky.org.uk

Scotch Whisky.net
www.scotchwhisky.net

Kentucky Bourbon Trail
www.kybourbontrail.com

There are numerous forums, blogs and vlogs on the internet, but these are some of the best:

Whisky Whisky Whisky
www.whiskywhiskywhisky.com

The Malt Maniacs
www.maltmaniacs.net

John Hansell
(the editor of *The Malt Advocate*)
www.whatdoesjohnknow.com

Ralf Mitchell's blog
www.ralfy.com

Serge Valentin's blog
www.whiskyfun.com

Glossary

Angels' share
As a cask of whisky matures, it loses liquid content and alcoholic strength through evaporation.

Backset
See sour mash

Beer still
The first still in American whiskey production, equivalent to the wash still in Scotch or Irish production.

Cask strength
The strength at which the whisky comes out of the cask(s) in which it has been ageing.

Chill-filtration
The removal of certain fats and tartrates (and also a little flavour) from the spirit at bottling by reducing the temperature to -4°C before bottling.

Direct fired
Most stills are heated by steam-filled coils within the still. Historically, they were direct fired, or heated by a fire lit underneath the still.

Draff
The solids remaining in the mash tun after the wort has been drained off. Draff is a high protein cattle fodder.

Finish
The practice of finalizing a whisky's maturation by filling the whisky into a different cask for the last of its ageing.

Green malt
The barley grain when it has been germinated.

Grist
The mixture of flour and husk ground from the dried green malt and cooked grains.

Low wines
The output from the first distillation in a pot still distillation, generally around 20 per cent ABV.

Lyne arm
The tube, attached to the top of a pot still, which carries the evaporate into a condenser or a worm tub.

Make
The general term given to the spirit produced in a distillery.

Mash
Mixture of grist and water heated to produce wort.

Mash bill
Grain recipe used by American distillers.

Pagoda heads
The distinctive feature on the roof of malt whisky distilleries. Nowadays, many are merely decorative, but their initial purpose was to draw the smoke up through the grain being dried in a kiln.

Pot ale
The liquid remaining in the wash still after the low wines have been drawn off. Also known as 'burnt ale', it is dried and used as animal fodder.

Small batch
Traditional definition: a bourbon that is produced/distilled in small quantities of approximately 1,000 gallons or less (20 barrels) from a mash bill of around 200 bushels of grain.

Sour mash
The habit of retaining a portion of the previous fermentation batch, together with its live yeast cells, which is added to the next run of mash, together with fresh yeast.

This helps the brewer to retain a consistent character in their wash.

Spent lees
Wash without alcohol, i.e. water and solids.

Staves
The strips of wood that make up the sides of a barrel or cask.

Top dressing
A single whisky of high quality, the addition of which to a blend raises the flavour of that blend to a higher level.

Uisge baugh
From the Scots Gaelic, meaning literally 'the water of life', but the spirit drunk pre-mid-18th century and generally mixed with herbs and/or spices to make a course spirit more palatable.

Uisge beatha
The Scots Gaelic 'water of life' drunk on its own or with a little water. *Uisce beatha* is the Gaelic equivalent.

Wash
The liquid obtained by fermenting wort with yeast, basically a high alcohol, hop-less beer that is destined for distillation in the wash still.

Wort
The hot, sweet liquid drawn off the draff in the mash tun, containing all the sugars from the grains.

Worm tubs
A large tub outside a distillery into which a coiled copper tube of decreasing diameter attached to the lyne arm of a pot still (the worm) sits. The worm tub contains running cold water and, inside it, the evaporate from the still condenses.

Index

This edition published by
Hardie Grant Books in 2016

Hardie Grant Books (UK)
52–54 Southwark Street
London SE1 1UN
hardiegrant.co.uk

Hardie Grant Books (Australia)
Ground Floor, Building 1
658 Church Street
Melbourne, VIC 3121
hardiegrant.com.au

Conceived and produced by
Elwin Street Productions Limited
14 Clerkenwell Green, London, EC1R 0DP
www.elwinstreet.com

British Library Cataloguing-in-Publication
Data. A catalogue record for this book is
available from the British Library.

Cover illustration: Clare Turner
Interior design: Fogdog.co.uk

ISBN: 978-1-78488-098-9

Printed in Malaysia

10 9 8 7 6 5 4 3 2 1

PICTURES: Aberlour Distillery, Banffshire,
UK, 30. Alamy Stock Photo: © 19th era 41;
© Age fotostock 52, 70; © Allan Munsie
50; © Amitav Ghosh 59; © Brent Hofacker
133; © Brian Jackson 13; © Chris George
82; © Christopher Jones 63; © Chronicle
26; © Daniel Dempster Photography 87; ©
David Burton 22; © David Gowans 31, 50;
© David Harding 54; © David Lyons 73; ©
Falkenstein/Bildagentur-online Historical
Collect. 74; © Hans Linden 17; © Hero
Images Inc 11; © Image Broker 78; © Jan
Holm 34; © Jeremy Sutton-Hibbert 115,
118, 127; © John Sylvester 104; © Malcolm
Gallon 43; © Malcro 12, 129; © Martin Grace
131; © MediaWorldImages 49, 107; © Niday
Picture Library 106; © OJO Images Ltd 7; ©
Parkerphotography 65; © Peter Horree 15,
67; © PhotoCuisine RM 121; © Plinthpics
135; © Samuel Whitton 95; © Stephen Finn
60; © Sue Heaton 77; © The Picture Pantry
101; © TNT Magazine 28, 53; © Tribune
Content Agency LLC 97; © Wanderluster 92;
© ZUMA Press Inc 37. Alberta Distillers Ltd,
Calgary, AB, Canada, 102. Amrut Distilleries,
Rajajinigar, Bangalore, 117. Auchentoshan
Distillery, Dalmuir, UK, 51. Old Bushmills
Distillery, County Antrim, UK, 75. Chichibu
Distillery, Saitama, Japan, 112. Compass Box
Whisky Co., London, UK, 66. Connemara
Cooley Distillery, County Louth, Ireland, 76.
Corbis: © CORBIS, 85; © Sandro Vannini/
CORBIS, 125; © Robert Wallis/Corbis, 68.
© Blaine Harrington III/Corbis, 91.. Crown
Royal Distillery, Gimli, Alberta, Canada,
103. Dalmore Distillery, Ross-shire, UK, 44.
Diageo UK: www.diageo.com, 128. Elijah
Craig/Heaven Hill Distillery, Bardstown, KY,
USA, 88. George Dickel Distillery, TN, USA,
96. Glendronach Distillery, Aberdeenshire,
UK, 45. Glendullan Distillery, Banffshire,
UK, 32. Glen Elgin Distillery, Elgin, UK, 33.
The Glenlivet Distillery, Banffshire, UK, 35.
Glenmorangie Distillery, Ross-shire, UK,
47. Green Spot/Pernod Ricard, 80. Hakushu
Higashi Distillery, Hokuto, Japan, 113. www.
riedel.co.uk, 25. ©2016 Jack Daniel's, Jack
Daniel Distillery, Lynchburg, TN, USA, 94.
The Kilbeggan Distilling Company, 81.
Knob Creek/Jim Beam Distillery, KY, USA,
86. Laphroaig Distillery, Isle of Islay, UK,
56. Longmorn Distillery, Moray, UK, 38.
Macallan Distillery, Moray, USA, 39. Macallan
Distillery, Moray, USA, 123. Mackmyra
Distillery, Valbo, Sweden, 111. Maker's
Mark Distillery, Loretto, KY, USA, www.
makersmark.com, 89. William Grant & Sons
Ltd, www.williamgrant.com, 61. Shutterstock
© Donfiore, 8; © Stockcreations, 8, 136.
Springbank Distillery, Campbeltown, UK, 57.
Tasmania Distillery, Cambridge, Tasmania/
sullivanscovewhisky.com, 116.